SILENT MOBIUS™

VOL. 2

This volume contains the monthly comics SILENT MÖBIUS PART 2 #1 through #5, PART 3 #1, and the first half of PART 3 #2 in their entirety.

STORY AND ART BY KIA ASAMIYA

ENGLISH ADAPTATION BY JAMES D. HUDNALL & MATT THORN

Touch-Up Art & Lettering/Wayne Truman
Cover Design/Hidemi Sahara
Editor/Jason Thompson

Director of Sales & Marketing/Oliver Chin
Managing Editor/Hyoe Narita
Editor-in-Chief/Satoru Fujii
Publisher/Seiji Horibuchi

Printed in Canada

Published by Viz Communications, Inc.
P.O. Box 77010 • San Francisco, CA 94107

10 9 8 7 6 5 4 3 2 1
First printing, April 1999

Vizit our web sites at **www.viz.com**, **www.pulp-mag.com**, **www.animerica-mag.com**, and our Internet magazine at **www.j-pop.com**!

VIZ GRAPHIC NOVEL

SILENT MÖBIUS™

VOL. 2

STORY AND ART BY

KIA ASAMIYA

CONTENTS

I'M NOT SURE THAT'S SUCH A GOOD THING.
THESE DAYS IT'S NOTHING BUT DESK WORK, HUH?
AT THIS RATE WE'RE GOING TO GET OUT OF SHAPE.
BACK-ACHES ALL THE TIME...
WITH THE CITY SO PEACE-FUL.
I GUESS SO...IT WOULD BE NICE IF IT COULD STAY THIS WAY.
WHAT ARE YOU TWO COMPLAINING ABOUT? IT'S A GOOD THING THAT A.M.P.'S NOT BUSY.

CHAPTER 04:
KATSUMI LIQUEUR

BUT PEACE IS SOMETHING THAT NEVER LASTS VERY LONG.

SO YOU'RE KATSUMI LIQUEUR.

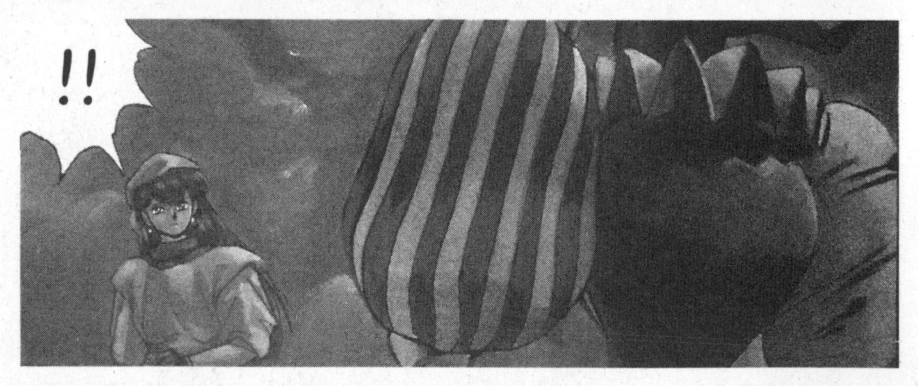

WHO...?
AH! KIDDY. LOOK, A NEW STORE--

YEAH, GREAT. YO, KATSUMI!
So you're the daughter of the great sorcerer Gigelf...

IT'S SPEAKING TO ME TELEPATHICALLY! WHO ARE YOU...?!

Heh...

I came all the way from the shadow world to see how great your powers really are.
ZEEE
Coke
WHAT?!
THEN YOU ARE...

YO, KATSUMI. LET'S CHECK OUT THIS STORE.
KATSUMI ?
VROOM
!
REALLY, KATSUMI-- WHAT'S WITH YOU? HAVING A STARING CONTEST WITH A CLOWN!
HEE HEE

HEY! KATSUMI! WHAT THE HELL --
KIDDY... GET AWAY. RUN.

WHAT...?
......
HURRY.

DOOM
TAMIYA
K'BLAM
WALK
STOP
KRAAK

P
FOOM
UWAH!
EAAH!
AARGH!!
WHAT ON EARTH IS GOING ON!?
SSSSHH

POLICE
!?
WHAT IS IT, CHIEF?
THIS SENSATION...
WHAT THE--!
WHAT ENTITY COULD EMANATE SUCH A STRONG AND OMINOUS ENERGY?

YE...YES, MA'AM.
TAKE CARE OF THE REST, LEBIA!
I'M GOING OUT!

YES, MA'AM.
AND CALL NAMI! HAVE HER AWAIT ORDERS AT HEADQUARTERS!

BEEP
HMPH-- THIS NEW ENTITY SEEMS TO HAVE A SERIOUS BLOODY ATTITUDE!
VEE E EE
F.A SHOOM
POLICE 65
KA SHHK
IT'S NOT TRYING TO HIDE ITS PRESENCE AT ALL. IT RADIATES IT TO THE MAX--
.....
VE E OOM
A TRAP...? INTERESTING.

What's wrong? Is that the BEST you can do?
Your father must be rolling over in his grave.

NO. CAN'T YOU SEE--?!
KATSUMI-- WHAT'S GOING ON!?
KATSUMI! YOU'RE ACTING WEIRD!

HOW CAN I DO THAT!? IT WILL MAKE ALL THESE PEOPLE DIE.
Feel free to chant your attack spell.
WEEOO WEEOO
WEEOO
WEEOO
all right, then...
SWOOSH
WAIT!!

SHOOM
WHAT IS THAT THING?
WHEW--
Fooled you.
WHOOSH
KIDDY! YUKI! GRAB ONTO ME! QUICK!
?
THWAK

WADO

OOOM

BBRRROOOOMM
RRRMMMBBB
WHOOO
WHAT... ?

Heh...
Aren't you going to thank me? Now you don't have to worry about innocent bystanders.
WHOOOOO

TCH!
Go ahead. Give me your best shot.

NOW JUST A SECOND--

Ah...
FWUMP
YUKI!

YOU...
YOU BASTARD!
go ahead and attack, Katsumi Liqueur!
HAHA HAHA HA

WHOOOOOO
Nnh!

Tch!
IF THE SHADOW DWELLERS REMEMBER MY NAME...
I MUST BE A BIG DEAL TO THEM, HUH...?
ALL RIGHT, THEN!
Thunder/lighening/come
Lash/burn/shatter--
Oh, come on. The THUNDER spell?!
You must be making fun of me.
WHA--
I HAVEN'T EVEN FINISHED...
I never expected such a low-level spell as a come back.
You could at least show me something...
FOOM

KRA
KOOM
...LIKE THIS!
WAH!
WADOOM
HA HA HA
EEEAH!

ZAAT
AAH!
BADOOM
WHUDD
Uhnn-
KATSUMI !?
I'm stunned. She can't even put up a barrier quickly enough.
She fell right into my wave spell. Hah!

HEY... KATSUMI! YOU ALL RIGHT?
NO. I'M NOT ALL RIGHT--
Nngh

WAAAA

HE'S PRETTY TOUGH, AIN'T HE?
KIDDY. YUKI. YOU'D BETTER GET AWAY WHILE YOU CAN.
HURRY!

WHAT'RE YOU TALKING ABOUT?!
IF I FAIL, YOU'LL ALL GO DOWN WITH ME. NOW HURRY, KIDDY. YOU TOO, YUKI!
BUT...
JUST DO IT!

KZZZZT
Stop talking!
WHAT'S WRONG, KATSUMI? GET SERIOUS!
KZZZT
SHUT UP!

SHEEE
KABOOM
KRAKK
RRMMBB

KADOOOM
WAKOOM
!!
AAH!

HFF...
THAT WAS TOO CLOSE.
......

KATSUMI...

Nngh!
THAK

VVOOO

VOOOOO
I'm waiting.
VEEEE
NOW IT'S MY TURN!

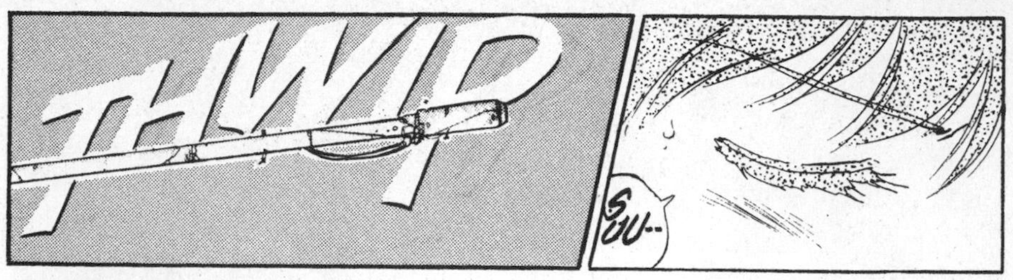
THWIP
S-UU--

HHMMMMM
Spirit of the dancing flame, grant
unto me a sword of explosive fire!
KK
KATSUMI! SHOW ME YOUR POWER!

KATSUMI! NO! STOP!
IT'S A TRAP!

KRAKO

OOOM

EEYAH!
K-KATSUMI!!
KDOOM

SSHHYUUU
BBUUM

RRMMBBLL

IS IT OVER...?
WOOOO

HYUUU
WHERE'S KATSUMI?

HAS THE EVIL ENTITY PHASED OUT?
HYUUU
AH...!
KATSUMI!!!

HYUO--
AH!
KATSUMI!
KATSUMI!
BEEP
THIS IS RALLY! SEND A RESCUE TEAM! URGENT!
CHIEF, IS KATSUMI...?
YES... THAT'S RIGHT.
SHE'S ALL RIGHT... I THINK.

WHAT DID THAT ENTITY WANT WITH KATSUMI?
STILL...
THANK GOODNESS.
HYUUU--

WOOO
She was taken down so easily, so quickly.
That girl...
Is she really the key? Can she really become the key?
HYUUU
!!
Mmm-- what an interesting young lady.
I'll have to pay a visit to her, sometime... heh heh heh...
!

HYUUUU
!

nuh
JUST NOW... I COULD HAVE SWORN...

WOOOO
Uhnn...
Uh...
-Ah-
oh...

KATSUMI!?
AH...
UM...
CALM DOWN, ROY...THEY'VE MANAGED TO PULL HER THROUGH.
--EH? WELL, THEN...
AH--
SHIK
......

CHIEF RALLY
WE'VE FINISHED, MORE OR LESS. HOWEVER, THE MENTAL DAMAGE WAS SO GREAT...
THE REST IS UP TO HER.
HMM... RIGHT. WHEN WILL SHE REGAIN CONSCIOUS-NESS?
PROBABLY SOMETIME TODAY OR TOMORROW...
POLICE
I SEE... BRING THE MEDICAL REPORT TO MY ROOM LATER.
YES, MA'AM.
THAT'S THE WAY IT IS, ROY. ARE YOU GOING TO STAY HERE WITH KATSUMI ?
NO... I'LL BE GOING BACK TO WORK.
POLICE

WHENEVER I LEAVE EARLY OR TAKE THE DAY OFF...
...SHE GETS REALLY MAD... AND SHE WORRIES SO...
POLICE
I SEE...
heh heh heh
BUT I'LL COME BY AND STAY WITH HER AS SOON AS MY SHIFT'S OVER.
ahem
EXIT
YOU DO THAT.
POLICE
KATSUMI...
SNARRK
YES, MA'AM!

--LAST NIGHT, DISTRICTS B-24 TO C-44...WHAT USED TO BE CALLED YOTSUYA TO ICHIGAYA...ARE IN A STATE OF ALMOST COMPLETE RUIN.
Katsumi's
THE POLICE HAVE RELEASED ABSOLUTELY NO DETAILS REGARDING THIS INCIDENT. PUBLIC OUTCRY IS GROWING.
HMM...
WHAT'S STOPPING OUR POLICE SPOKESMEN FROM SAYING THAT AN ENTITY DID IT?
LIGHTEN UP, KIDDY.
THERE ARE ALWAYS THOSE WHO'RE BLAMED AND THOSE WHO BLAME. IT'S THE BUSINESS.
I DON'T BUY THAT.
WHAT ?!
SIGH
YOU SURE ARE DENSE.

TRY SAYING THAT AGAIN !
SHOOM
YOU'RE ALWAYS LIKE THIS. ACTING LIKE YOU KNOW EVERYTHING !
OKAY. YOU'RE DENSE.
WHAMMM
KRNCH
SO ?
HOW CAN YOU. BE SO CALM, LEBIA?
THE PUBLIC IS YELLING AT THE POLICE, AND THE POLICE CAN'T SAY ANYTHING. MANY IN THE DEPARTMENT ARE EVEN LOOKING AT US WITH SUSPICION.
DOESN'T THAT BOTHER YOU AT ALL?
BEFORE YOU GET SO MAD, AREN'T THERE SOME THINGS WE NEED TO DO FIRST?

HAH! THE WAY THINGS ARE NOW, JUST WHAT CAN A.M.P. DO?! EVEN YOU, LEBIA--
WHAP
LEBIA-A-A-A!
GRRR
YOU!
WHOOSH
MPD
YES, YES! YOU'RE NOT A CHILD, SO STOP ACTING LIKE ONE.
AH!

KAWAKK
THOOM
MEMO
.....
...OOPS...!
WHAT DO YOU MEAN "OOPS"!?
WERE YOU TRYING TO KILL ME ?!

IF THAT'S WHAT YOU WANT...
STOP THIS! RIGHT NOW!
WHAT'S THE MATTER WITH YOU TWO? KATSUMI'S IN THE HOSPITAL, AND YOU'RE ACTING LIKE LUNATICS!
SNOORK
WAAAAH

.....
snff snff
MY, MY... WHEN DID THE A.M.P. BECOME AN ELEMENTARY SCHOOL?
AND TO THINK WE JUST HAD IT REMODELED.
LEBIA, COME TO MY OFFICE WHEN YOU'RE DONE HERE. I WANT YOU TO EXPLAIN JUST WHAT WENT ON HERE.
Y-YES, MA'AM.
AH-- THIS WAS... UH...

That won't be necessary...

WAAAUH
I'M SO BO-O-O-RED!
OH, WELL, I GUESS THAT'S WHAT BEING LAID UP IS ALL ABOUT.
TIK
BUT THERE'S NOTHING ELSE TO DO.
TIK
BEEP
I KNOW WATCHING TV IS DULL
VMMMMM
HUH?
I HAVEN'T SELECTED A CHANNEL YET, BUT...
--CONTRACT OF BLOOD--
--INHERIT ME--
WHAT IS...

HMMMMM
ABIDE BY THE CONTRACT OF BLOOD...
...AND INHERIT ME.
CHK
VVVT
OH, NO--!
MIND CONTROL--!?
ABIDE BY THE CONTRACT OF BLOOD AND INHERIT ME!
WHO WOULD'VE THOUGHT... IT COULD ENTER THROUGH THE TV CIRCUIT?
WHO IS IT? IT COULDN'T BE...?
ABIDE BY THE CONTRACT OF BLOOD AND INHERIT ME!
ENTI-
-TY...?
ABIDE BY THE CONTRACT OF BLOOD AND INHERIT ME!!

PSSH
TP

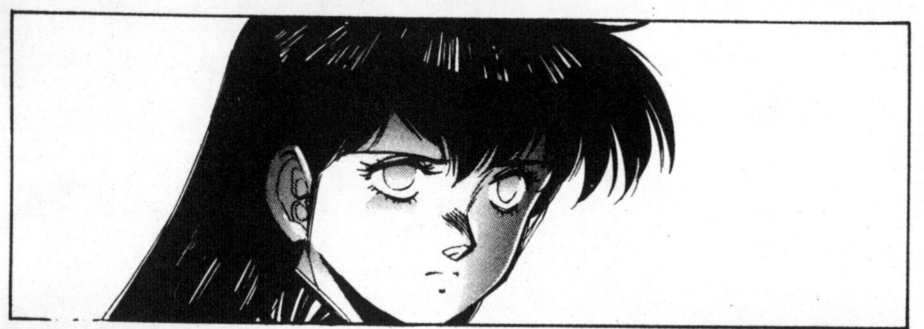
ZZZZZT

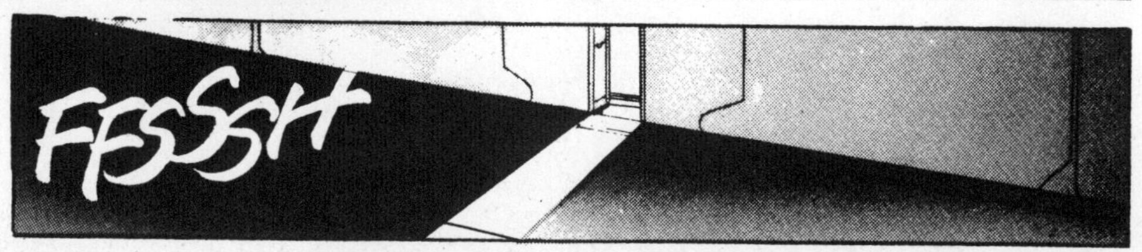
FFSSSH

FASHNN
HI! HOW'VE YOU BEEN, HUEY?
JING
VOICEPRINT CHECK CONFIRMS YOU ARE KATSUMI LIQUEUR.
I'VE BEEN FINE, MORE OR LESS.
BEEP
I'M GOING TO BORROW YOU FOR A BIT.
BUT MY MASTER IS LEBIA MAVERICK AND--
IF YOU'RE THINKING OF LEBIA, DON'T WORRY...I'VE ALREADY TALKED WITH HER.
VRRM
I NEED YOU TO GO...

MS. LIQUEUR, YOUR BRAINWAVES... ARE THE SAME AS WHEN YOU'RE ASLEEP.
WA
SUZUKI
VUMMM
DON'T WORRY ABOUT IT.
PARDON ME.
RIGHT. THAT'S JUST FINE.
VOOOOM
MS. LIQUEUR ?
PING
PING

BUT... IT'S ODD.
AROOM
HUEY! IF YOU MENTION IT AGAIN, I'LL GET MAD!
WHAT...?
YOU'RE LISTED AS BEING ADMITTED TO THE POLICE HOSPITAL. WHY ARE YOU--
!!
HOW MUCH LONGER TO OUR DESTINATION?
WAAAAH
...FIVE MINUTES, MA'AM...
CHAK
GOOD BOY.

YOU!
Heh, heh, heh... I know you two, but this is the first time I've met the others.
I wonder what rank you humans have given me?
Middle?
Or upper class? ...Heh, heh...
IT CAME RIGHT INTO A.M.P.!
I CAN'T BELIEVE IT! POLICE HEAD-QUARTERS--
WE'RE SUPPOSED TO BE PROTECTED BY MANY LAYERS OF SPIRIT SHIELDS. HOW?
Humans have such amazing confidence in their devices. Are you saying your spirit shields are flawless?
How naive.

Your shields are useless against me.
HAH HAH HAH HAH
Understand?
WHAT'S YOUR PURPOSE IN COMING HERE?
Purpose?
Why... to kill you all, of course. And to see what Rally Cheyenne...
...is made of.
!
THAT'S COMING FROM HUEY...
SOMEONE'S DRIVING HUEY...?
BEEP
PING
VOOOOO
Prepare to die!
SWHOOSH
KKKZZZTT

--ABIDE BY THE CONTRACT OF BLOOD AND INHERIT ME--

WHERE AM I ?!
HYUUUO O
WHY AM I DRESSED THIS WAY? I SHOULD BE IN THE HOSPITAL.
HYUUUOO
HUEY? WHAT'S LEBIA'S BIKE DOING HERE?
MS. LIQUEUR ?
HYUUUOOOOO
IT WAS YOU WHO BROUGHT ME HERE. WASN'T IT ?
IT SEEMS YOU WERE HYPNOTIZED BY SOMEONE, DOESN'T IT?
WHAT ?
YES! ONLY BECAUSE YOU THREATENED ME WITH YOUR GUN.

ABIDE BY THE CONTRACT OF BLOOD AND INHERIT ME.
HYUUOO
MY NAME IS GROSPOLINER, THE KING OF SWORDS.
!!

WHAT...
HYUUOOO
.....
ABIDE BY THE CONTRACT OF BLOOD AND INHERIT ME.
SHAKOW
...IS THIS ?!
UH!

OW-W-W-W!

YOU'RE... AN ENTITY!
YOU BASTARD!
I AM NOT AN ENTITY.
NO.
HYUOO
NOW THEN, KATSUMI LIQUEUR, GIVE YOUR BLOOD TO THIS MONUMENT.
THAT IS THE CONTRACT OF BLOOD.
MY... BLOOD?!
BUT YOUR VOICE, YOUR TACTICS... THEY'RE LIKE AN ENTITY'S.

...O DAUGHTER OF MY MASTER.
I WANT TO BE FREE...

HYUUOOOO
"MY MASTER"?
"DAUGHTER"?
MY FATHER? YOU ARE TALKING ABOUT MY FATHER, AREN'T YOU!?
THAT IS CORRECT. MY MASTER, GIGELF LIQUEUR.
THAP
TELL ME! TELL ME ABOUT MY FATHER!
I WANT TO KNOW EVERYTHING... ALL ABOUT HIM.
EVERYTHING...
WOOOOO

MY FATHER... BY THE TIME I WAS BORN, HE WAS ALREADY DEAD.
I ONLY HEARD ABOUT HIM FROM MY MOTHER.
I ALWAYS WONDERED WHAT KIND OF PERSON HE WAS.
I ONLY KNOW HIM FROM STORIES, LEGENDS.
BUT NOW, FATHER IS BECOMING MORE AND MORE CONNECTED TO ME.
ENTITIES...
MYSELF...
THIS WORLD...
HAVE I BEEN WAITING FOR...
THIS DAY?
SOB
I HAVE, TOO, KATSUMI LIQUEUR.

...WAITED FOR THE DAY YOU BECAME AN ADULT AND DEVELOPED ENOUGH POWER...
TO INHERIT ME!
WHAT?
...WAITED FOR THE DAY WHEN YOU WOULD TAKE UP YOUR FATHER'S MANTLE AND ACCEPT MY SERVICES.
TAKE THE PLACE OF MY FATHER...
AND INHERIT YOU...?
I HAVE WAITED FOR THIS DAY. TWENTY-TWO YEARS TO BE EXACT...
YES. YOU ARE TO BECOME MY MASTER...
KATSUMI LIQUEUR.

YOU HAVE ONLY TO PLACE A LITTLE OF YOUR BLOOD ONTO THE CROSS BELOW.
WHEN I'VE CONFIRMED THAT BLOOD, THE CONTRACT WILL BE COMPLETE.
HOLD IT...
......
AN INCREDIBLY POWERFUL ENTITY COULD BE INSIDE THIS TOWER.
THIS IS...
...A TRAP!
H YUUOO
IF IT WAS MY FATHER WHO LOCKED IT IN, MY BLOOD COULD FREE IT.
HAH HAH HAH HAH!!

HA HA... EXCUSE ME...
IT'S JUST THAT YOUR SKEPTICISM REMINDED ME OF YOUR FATHER.
WH-WHAT'S SO FUNNY?
MY FATHER...?
BELIEVE ME, KATSUMI LIQUEUR. I AM NOT AN ENTITY.

.....OKAY.
CNCH

WHO
DIIIEE!!!
DIE NOW!!
SHOOOOM

KZZAAT
OOSH

!
HUH ?
NOTHING HAPPENED...
!!!
My dark power was... eliminated !
Impossible !
The defenses of this police station couldn't have such power...
And yet.

Rally Cheyenne! It was you, wasn't it?
AND IF IT WAS...?
.....
YOUR POWERS ARE USELESS.
YUKI! LEBIA! READY GRAVITONS!
YES, MA'AM!
FIRE!
AMPD

KOOM
KOOM
VEEEE
Wuh--
BDOOOM
SHU UUM

VVMMMMM
Pish
Pat
Heh heh heh...
That won't work!
SSHHHH
Try another trick!
?!
YOU SAID YOU WANTED TO SEE WHAT I AM MADE OF...
SO I'LL SHOW YOU. MY POWER, THAT IS.

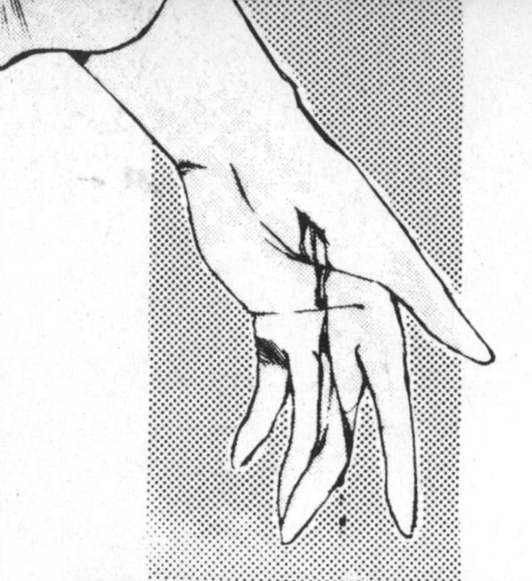

WOOO
OOOO

!
KRKK
KRKK
KRAAKK

STAY AWAY, KATSUMI !
WH... WHAT ?
KRIK
KRAK
RRMMBBL

KRAK
KRKK
KRKK
KRKK

KOOM
WHAT'S...

WHOOM
WHAT ON EARTH?
A SWORD?
WOW!
KA-SHING
FUMP
WHOA...

HYUOOO
WHAT IS THIS... ?

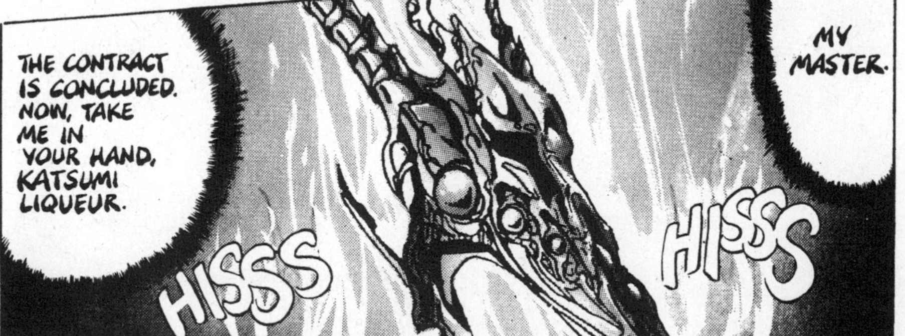
MY MASTER.
THE CONTRACT IS CONCLUDED. NOW, TAKE ME IN YOUR HAND, KATSUMI LIQUEUR.
HISSS
HISSS

TAKE YOU IN MY HAND ?!
YOU MUST WEIGH A TON!
KREEEK
!!

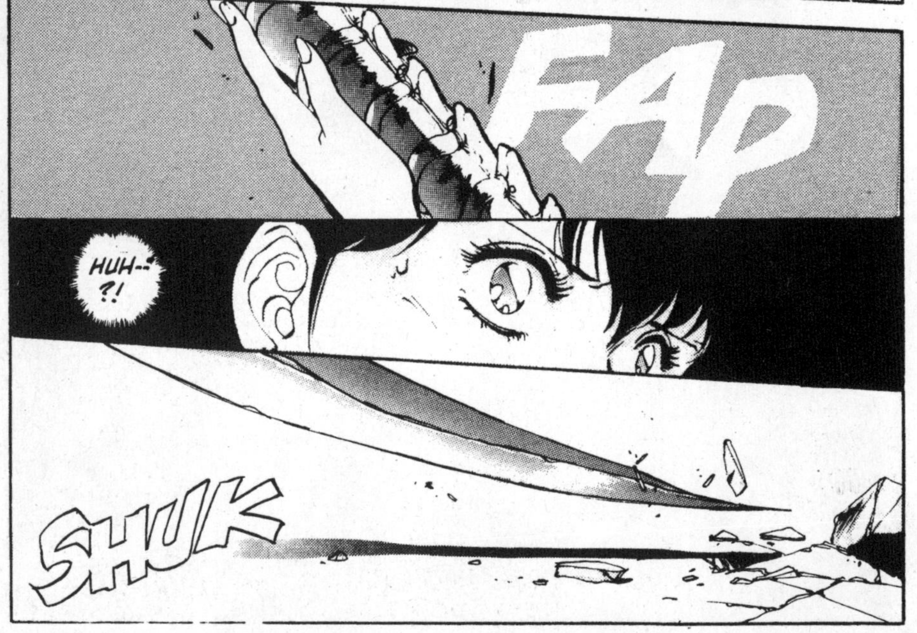
FAP
HUH--?!
SHUK

I CAN'T BELIEVE...
IT'S SO...
LIGHT.

THERE'S NOTHING STRANGE ABOUT IT.
THROUGH THE CONTRACT OF BLOOD, I RECEIVED YOUR BLOOD AND I AM NOW A PART OF YOUR BODY.

YOU DON'T FEEL THE WEIGHT OF YOUR LIMBS WHEN YOU MOVE THEM, DO YOU?
IT'S THE SAME THING.

WELL, MASTER, SHALL WE GO?
GO...?
DON'T YOU SENSE THE EXTRAORDINARY VIBRATIONS COMING FROM YOUR POLICE DEPARTMENT?

!

HUEY!
YES?
TCH. TCH.

WHY WERE YOU LOCKED UP IN THERE ?

VROOM

THAT TOWER WAS A MONUMENT. A CERTAIN PLAN FAILED, YOU SEE.

I WAS PLACED THERE BY ONE OF THE ENTITIES.

HMMM...

IN ORDER TO BREAK THE SEAL, IT WOULD TAKE THE SAME BLOOD AS MY MASTER'S.

THE BLOOD OF THE SUPER-SORCERY CLAN.

WAAAAOOO

SORCERY... CLAN?

KATSUMI, HAVE YOU EVER THOUGHT ABOUT WHAT WE CALL MAGIC?

VAARROOM

MAGIC?
THAT'S RIGHT. ...YOU COULD THINK OF MAGIC AS THE COMMON ORDER OF A DIFFERENT PLANE. THE SIMPLE PHYSICS OF ANOTHER WORLD.
WHEN THIS ORDER APPEARS IN A DIFFERENT WORLD, LIKE THIS ONE, IT BECOMES AN UNUSUAL POWER.
AND THAT'S... MAGIC?
RECENTLY THE DOORS BETWEEN THIS WORLD AND NEMESIS, THE EVIL SPIRIT WORLD, WERE OPENED.
BUT THESE DOORS HAVE NOT OPENED COMPLETELY.
THAT'S WHY THE ENTITIES MUST APPROXIMATE THE LAWS OF THIS SIDE WHEN THEY COME HERE.
AH!

I SEE... THEIR BODIES TAKE ON AN ALMOST HUMAN FORM, RIGHT?
CORRECT.
WELL, THEN... WHAT ABOUT MY FATHER'S MAGIC?

THOUGH THE DOORS HAVE RECENTLY BEEN OPENED, THIS IS NOT THE FIRST TIME THE ENTITIES HAVE COME HERE.
WAAOOO
THERE IS PLENTY OF EVIDENCE THAT SHOWS ENTITIES HAD, SHALL WE SAY, RELATIONS WITH HUMANS IN ANCIENT TIMES.
THUS YOUR POWERS OF MAGIC ARE THE LEGACY OF YOUR BLOOD.
!
YOU MEAN, SOME OF MY ANCESTORS WERE ENTITIES ?!
HA HA-- BUT IT WAS HUMANS WHO POLISHED THAT POWER THEMSELVES...
PING
...IN THEIR QUEST TO ACHIEVE GREATER POWER.
PING
VROOOM
BY THE WAY, IT SEEMS WE AREN'T HEADED FOR POLICE HEADQUARTERS.
THE MIXING OF ENTITY BLOOD WITH THAT OF HUMANS WAS ONLY THE BEGINNING.
YOUR STORY GIVES ME MIXED EMOTIONS.
YEAH. I'VE GOT TO GET SOMETHING AT HOME FIRST.

I will return to my original form!
Fine! I can't maintain this form much longer anyway!
VEEEEEE
DOWN, EVERYONE!

BDOOM

RRMMBB
WHAT... ?!
YAAH !
Hah hah hah! Why don't you show me now, Rally Cheyenne!? Show me your power!

SO YOU ARE MID-LEVEL AFTER ALL.
What?! You'll regret that!

CHIEF!
SCREECH
SORRY I'M LATE. IT'S KATSUMI!
BRROOOM
TAP
KATSUMI! YOU'RE THE ONE WHO WAS RIDING HUEY WITHOUT MY PERMISSION!
HMM... THAT SWORD!

YOU'VE GOT SOME NERVE BREAKING IN HERE, YOU NETHERWORLD CLOWN!

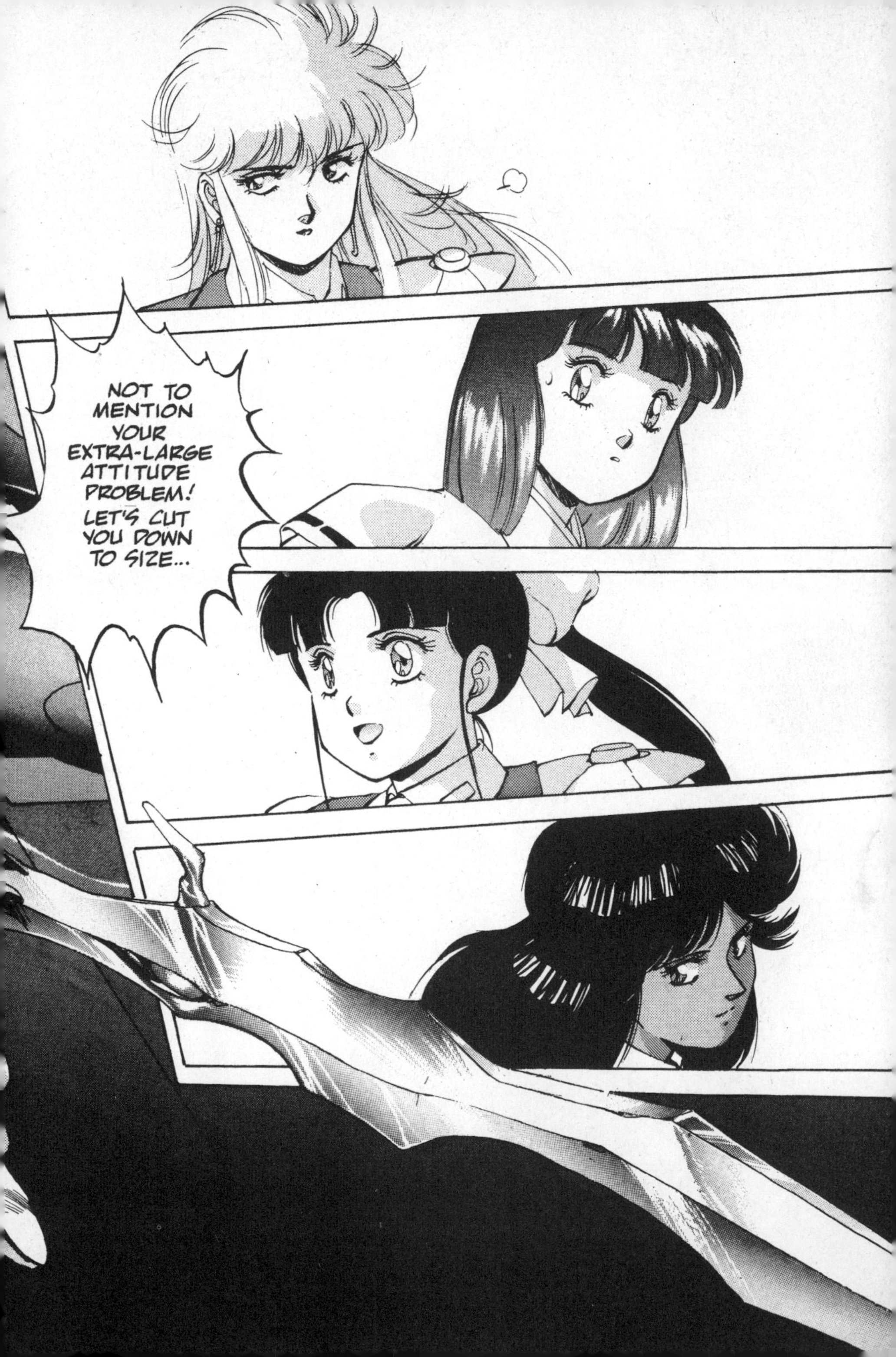
NOT TO MENTION YOUR EXTRA-LARGE ATTITUDE PROBLEM!
LET'S CUT YOU DOWN TO SIZE...

...AND THIS SWORD IS JUST THE WEAPON TO DO IT!
WHOOSH
SAY YOUR PRAYERS!
The impudence of this brat! Feel my power!
KKZZZZT
Wha-a-a-at!?
WABOOM
KRAKOOM

WHOOSH
EEAAAH!
AAH!

That sword! It can't be!
Grospoliner, king of all swords!
Impossible!!

You've been freed? From there?
YES! WE MEET AGAIN, MOVA de BADINA!

RRR--if so, it's time for a change of plans.
I'm moving the battleground somewhere else.
I can't fight you on even terms in this spirit shield.

WA
HE'S DISAPPEARED!
HYUUOOOO
HE BROKE THE SPIRIT SHIELD WITH THAT EXPLOSION AND ESCAPED!
DAMN!
WAIT, KATSUMI! FOR GOODNESS' SAKE, CHANGE YOUR CLOTHES! THIS IS SERIOUS WORK!
KATSUMI...
ALL RIGHT, ALL RIGHT!
HE SHOULD BE IN TOWN SOMEWHERE. BRING HIM DOWN BEFORE HE RUNS AMOK!
YES, MA'AM.
YES, MA'AM!

BOOM
CHIEF...I HAVE A BAD... PREMONITION.
I CAN'T SEE THE POLICE BUILDING HERE TOMORROW.
WHAT?
WE SHOULD EVACUATE THE WHOLE STAFF RIGHT AWAY.
.....
RIGHT! GET ON THE PHONE AND SEE TO IT THAT HEADQUARTERS AND THE SUR-ROUNDING AREA ARE EVACUATED.
YES, MA'AM!

HYOOOO
WNWNN
So you've come, Katsumi Liqueur!
Both you and your sword shall be ground into dust.
WRONG, BOZO! YOUR CHOICE OF BATTLEGROUNDS MAKES MY JOB MUCH EASIER!
Think again, fool! I just didn't want any interference.
FOOM
I'M RETURNING ALL THE PAIN YOU GAVE ME! IN SPADES!

BRINGS BACK MEMORIES, MOVA! WE'VE CROSSED THIS WAY IN THE PAST!
KLANK
KLANK
Yes, Grospoliner! It certainly does! That it should end for good just now--
is too bad!
SHWAK
EYAHH!
KATSUMI! DON'T GET EXCITED! A BEGINNER LIKE YOU HAS NO HOPE OF BEATING HIM WITH SWORDSMANSHIP ALONE!
THAK
I KNOW THAT! WHAT AM I SUPPOSED TO DO?!
SWOOSH

You have yet to master the use of Grospoliner, I see!
THAP
Tch!
KATSUMI! DON'T TRY TO FIGHT WITH SWORDS ALONE!
FOOM
YOU MUST CALL UPON THE HEAVENLY POWERS OF THE CELESTIAL BODIES, AS I TAUGHT YOU EARLIER.
THAT'S EASY FOR YOU TO SAY, BUT...
Lecturing at a time like this?
SHOOM
Too Late!!
AS LONG AS YOU DON'T USE SWORD AND MAGIC TOGETHER, YOU WILL FAIL.
KLANG
I KNOW, ALREADY!

HYUUOOO
Tck!
Where are you?
ADOOM
REMEMBER, KATSUMI! WHAT I TAUGHT YOU EARLIER!
YEAH.
WAAOOO
HEAVENLY SPIRITS?
THAT'S RIGHT. THE SPIRITS THAT RESIDE IN THE THIRTEEN ANCIENT CELES-TIAL BODIES.
THE PLANET SPIRIT HAS TREMENDOUS POWER AND INFLUENCE AGAINST WHICH THE OTHER SPIRITS CANNOT COMPARE.
YOU KNOW THAT SPIRITS RESIDE IN ALL MATTER ON THE FACE OF THIS EARTH. THERE IS EVEN A SPIRIT RESIDING IN THE EARTH ITSELF.
SUZUKI

YOUR MAGIC NOW CALLS UPON NOTHING MORE THAN MINOR SPIRITS.
WAAOOOO
NOT GOOD ENOUGH, HUH?
NO! YOU CANNOT CONFRONT THE POWER OF THIS ENTITY WITH THAT ALONE!

TEACHING YOU SUCH THINGS IS ONE OF THE ROLES ENTRUSTED TO ME BY YOUR FATHER, MASTER GIGELF.
MY FATHER?

THE POWER OF A HEAVENLY SPIRIT IS DIRECTLY RELATED TO ITS POSITION. IT IS IMPERATIVE THAT YOU ALWAYS KNOW WHERE THE STARS AND PLANETS ARE.
WAAOOO
OH, COME ON...
NEVER MIND. NOW I WILL TEACH YOU THE SPELLS OF SUMMONING, STARTING WITH SOL...

WAAOOO
LET'S GO, KATSUMI!
GOT IT!
Stop hiding and come out!
Katsumi Liqueur!

Is your lecture finished? Here I come, Katsumi!
FINE! I'M READY!
FOOM
SHEEN
Spirits of Sol and Mars, known as Solal and Barzabel! Grant the power of gold and steel to my sword! I am in the bosom of Gaea!
What!?
VEEEE

KA
SHANG
Gyah!
BOOOM
Gah!
ALL RIGHT!
It can't be! This power--! It's as if...
It's the same power as the great sorcerer, Gigelf Liqueur!
SPOOK SPUT

LET'S FINISH HIM OFF!
THAP THAP THAP
VOOM
If you can, that is!
WHOOM
KADOOM
EEAHH!
WHAT'S THAT?
LOOK OUT!

HYWOOO
Coca-Cola
Lose? am I to lose? Me?!
Unnggh
I, with whom even Gigelf Liqueur was evenly matched?
FINISH HIM, KATSUMI!
VMMM
Spirits of the sky, Shad Bal'shmos Haa of the moon! Cast on me the silver sword! Shed the light meant for the planet Thune! And fulfill the contract with Selene.
Y-YEAH!
I won't die alone!
Uhnn...

KBOOM
SHAKOOM
GYAH!

FWOOSH
VEEEE

FW
BOOM

TH-- THEY'VE NEGATED THE MAGIC!
!!
IT SEEMS YOUR BLOODLINE IS STILL VERY POTENT.
JUST WHAT WE SHOULD HAVE EXPECTED FROM YOU, MISS LIQUEUR.

AND YOU TRIED TO KILL THAT WOMAN...
SHE IS A LIVING "KEY." SHE CAN FULLY OPEN THE DOORS BETWEEN NEMESIS AND THIS WORLD.
WHAT... ?
Who... are... you...?
G- Guh-

WHO ARE YOU? WHAT... ARE YOU?
A HUMAN...
...ON THE SIDE OF NEMESIS.
WHA...?
TO DEFEAT HUMANS, ONE MUST KNOW THEIR STRENGTHS AND WEAKNESSES INTIMATELY.
JUST AS YOU A.M.P. WOMEN USE MAGIC TO DEFEAT ENTITIES.
VOOM
BEGONE, LOWLY ANIMAL!

DON'T BE SURPRISED.
IT'S NOT SO RARE A THING.
VE E E E E
!?

AT ANY RATE, WE'VE LOST ONE OF OURS...
SO IT'S ONLY FAIR WE RETURN THE FAVOR.
SNAP

FWOOSH
AXIA

KRAKKK
VAWOOM
BBDDDUUMMM

POLICE HEADQUARTERS
!

DON'T WORRY. NO ONE WAS INSIDE.
NOW THEN...IT'S ABOUT TIME FOR US TO WITHDRAW.
NEXT TIME WE COME, WE'LL TAKE *YOU*.

!
AH, ALSO, IT SEEMS YOU HAVE A LOVER.
HE IS IN OUR WAY!

WHAT... ?!

POP

.....
HYUOOO

AHCHOO!

RCA

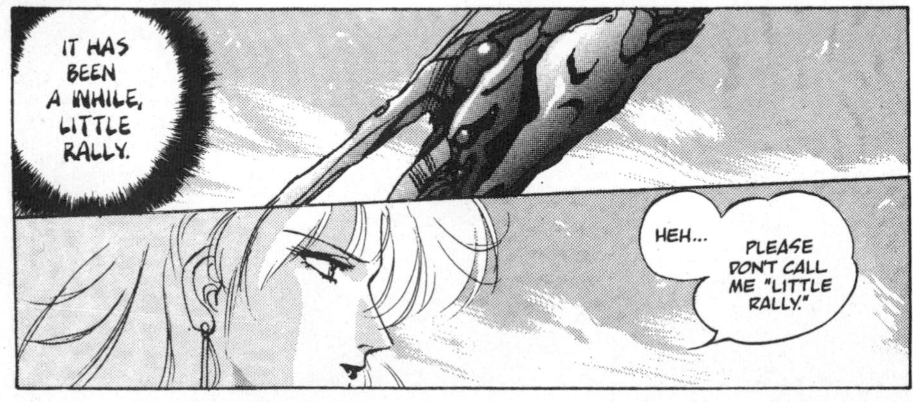
IT HAS BEEN A WHILE, LITTLE RALLY.
HEH... PLEASE DON'T CALL ME "LITTLE RALLY."

CHAPTER 05:
YUKI SAIKO

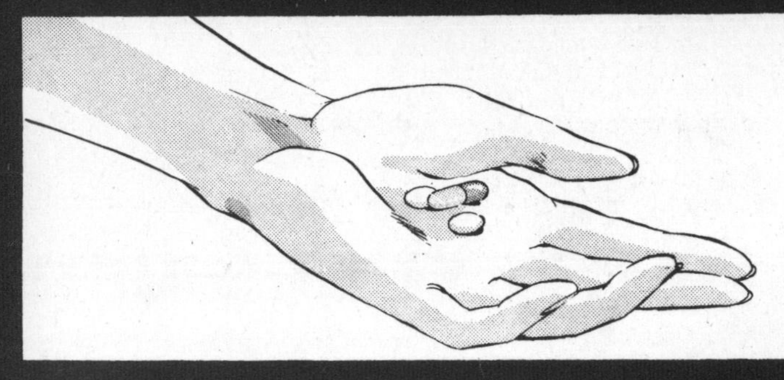
HERE YOU GO, YUKI. SAY Ahhh.

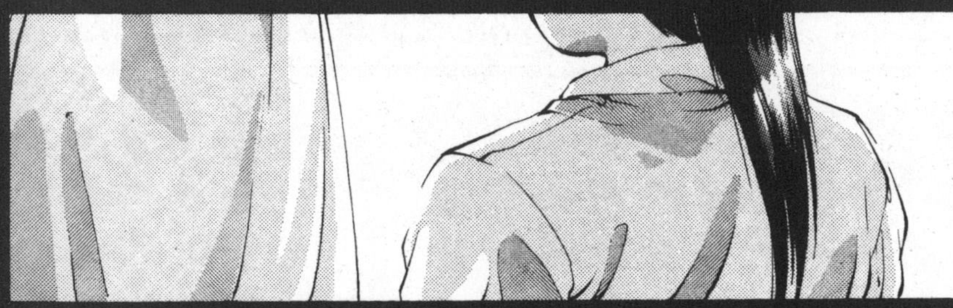

WHAT'S WRONG ?
I DON'T WANNA. DON'T LIKE MED'CIN.

BUT YOUR FRIENDS...
THEY'RE TAKING THEIRS.

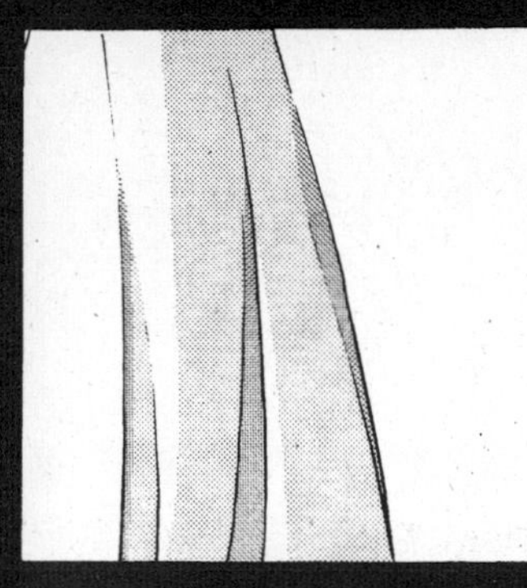
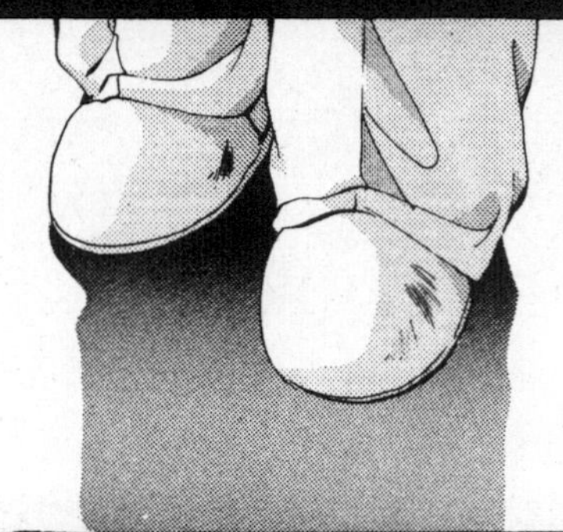
NO! I DON'T WANT IT!

WHAT'S THE PROBLEM ?
OH, MY...

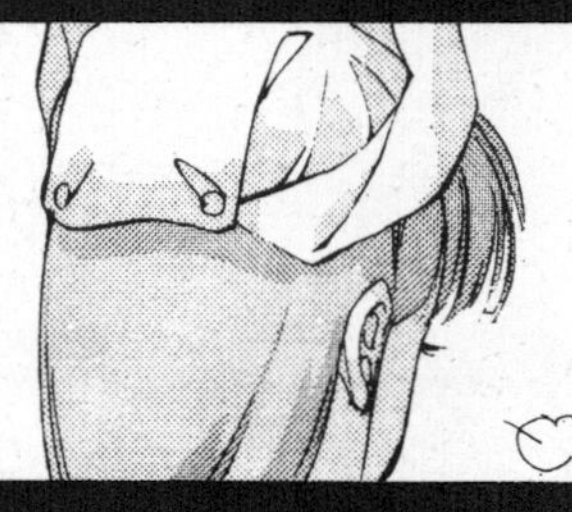

B-007... I MEAN, YUKI WON'T...
OH, DOCTOR...

IF YOU DON'T TAKE THESE, YOU WON'T GET BIG.
HMM... YUKI, WHY WON'T YOU TAKE YOUR MEDICINE ?

BUT IF YOU DON'T TAKE THIS, YOU WON'T BECOME STRONG.

STRONG...

A.M.P.'s RANKING: LOW ENTITIES HAVE LOW INTELLIGENCE.

IDIOT!
BOOM
SHWOOM

KATSUMI!

BUDOOMBUDOOM
GWAH!
SHLUOOP
SHLUOOP

SSSHHH
BEEP
DID YOU FINISH IT OFF? IT SEEMS THE SIGNAL'S DISAPPEARED... YUKI?
.....
GLOOP

!!

I... I'M NO GOOD. I'M BECOMING A BURDEN TO EVERYONE.

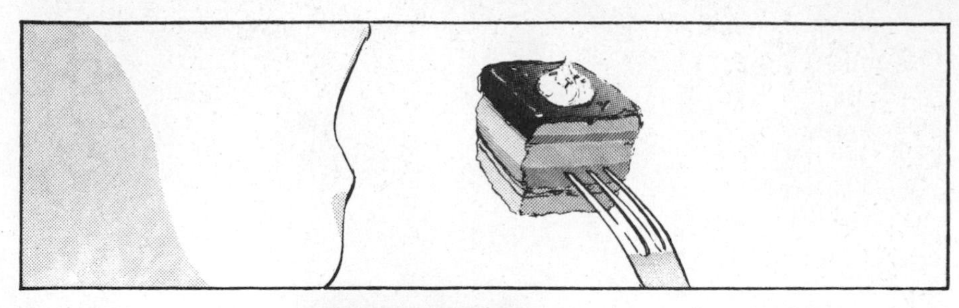

U...
A...
IT'S SO SWE-E-E-E-T!

FLING
gag?

BUT ISN'T IT... EXTREME?
OF COURSE IT'S SWEET. IT'S CAKE!

OH, WELL. I GUESS I JUST DON'T HAVE A SWEET TOOTH.
Hah

YOU CAN'T TAKE SPICY THINGS EITHER.

WHAT?
WHAT?

Munch
NOW THAT YOU MENTION IT, YUKI'S COFFEE SHOP DOESN'T HAVE ANY CAKE, DOES IT?

HA HA--THAT'S BECAUSE YUKI CAN'T BAKE CAKES.
AT ALL.
HUH...
BUT SHE COULD ORDER CAKES, COULDN'T SHE?

NO WAY. WITH YUKI, EVERYTHING HAS TO BE HOMEMADE.
Ha ha ha
YEAH. THE ONLY THING ON THE MENU IS COFFEE.
HMMM...

I GUESS I JUST WANT PEOPLE...
...TO HAVE SOMETHING WARM AND HOMEMADE.
.....
WELL, IT'S HALF HOBBY, ANYWAY, SO WHY DOES IT MATTER?
...SHE SAYS.
WHICH MUST MEAN HER COFFEE SHOP MUST NOT BE MAKING MUCH MONEY.
WHO KNOWS WHEN SHE'LL EVER START SERVING FOOD.

VOOOOOO
BEEP BEEP

♪

SPLISH
SPLOSH
WOOOOO
SIGH
TP
PING

......
SIX...

I'VE GAINED SIX POUNDS!

WHAT'LL I DO...
WHAT'LL I DO...
WHAT'LL I DO...
WHAT'LL I DO...
TH-THAT'S IT--
I'LL GO ON A DIET!
CAN'T EAT ANYTHING...
ESPECIALLY HIGH-CALORIE FOODS.
TADA!
TADA!
TADA!

DIET?
AND YOU HAVEN'T HAD ANYTHING BUT WATER AND APPLES IN THE LAST THREE DAYS?
YEAH.
WHAT?! WHAT'S SO FUNNY!?
HEE HEE HEE
WHY DON'T YOU JUST TAKE A WEIGHT CONTROL CAPSULE? IT'S THE 21ST CENTURY, SILLY!
CAPSULE...

NO!!
IF YOU DON'T LIKE THAT, THEY CAN EXTRACT YOUR FAT WITH A--
Sob Sob
HUH?
NO...
!
NO...
WHA...
NO!
sniff sniff
NO.
NO.
AH!
WHAT IS IT, YUKI?
YUKI...?

!
GRUMBL L
!?

Badump
Badump
Badump
UH... YUKI... ?
.....

OOOH-- KATSUMI, KIDDY, LEBIA--
I HATE YOU ALL !!

THAT WAS MY STOMACH THAT GROWLED.
I HAVEN'T EATEN ALL DAY AND...

HEY!

.....
YUKI...
--FOR CRYIN' OUT LOUD, KATSUMI, YOU DO THE STUPIDEST THINGS!
BUT STILL...
I CAN'T WAIT TO GET OUT OF THIS TEMPORARY STATION.
WHEN ARE THEY GONNA FINISH THE NEW PLACE, ANYWAY?
DON'T CHANGE THE SUBJECT!

CHIEF !!
!
UH... UM...
YUKI...?
AM I... WHAT AM I DOING HERE?
CHIEF, WHY DID YOU HAVE ME JOIN THE A.M.P.?
IT SEEMS LIKE... LIKE I'M GETTING IN EVERYONE'S WAY...
IF... IF I'M SOMETHING LIKE A MASCOT FOR A.M.P....
THEN I... I WON'T...

I JUST WON'T STAND FOR IT !!
YUKI... ?
YUKI !!
WUMPF
YUKI !

--JUST... JUST WHAT AM I TO A.M.P.? HAVE I SERVED ANY PURPOSE?
WHY DID CHIEF RALLY MAKE ME A MEMBER?
TELL ME...
SOMEBODY...
ANYBODY...
--AM I REALLY JUST A MASCOT?
I FEEL SAD...
SO SAD...

KATSUMI AND KIDDY HAVE INCREDIBLE POWER.
AND LEBIA IS SO BEAUTIFUL...
AND NAMI, TOO...
I...

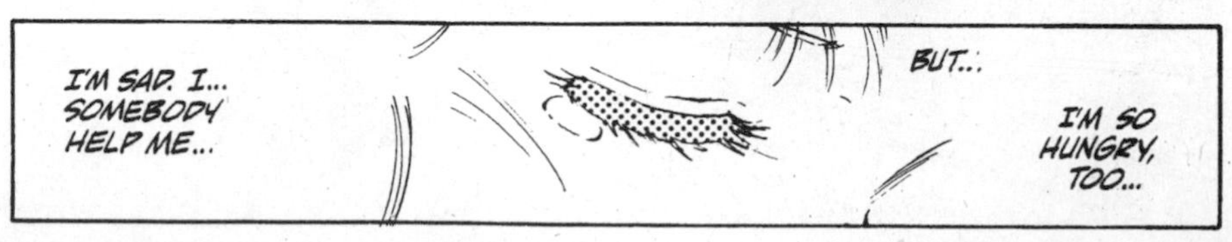
I'M SAD. I... SOMEBODY HELP ME...
BUT...
I'M SO HUNGRY, TOO...

Uh...
Mm...
Aa...

HUH...

WHERE...?
IT'S MY... ROOM.

FWMP
Mm

SIGH

AHHH... I WANT TO BE AN ADULT.
I WONDER IF I'LL BE LIKE KATSUMI?
OR PRETTY LIKE LEBIA...?
I REALLY WANT TO GROW UP QUICKLY.

HUH?

COCONUTS
CORN SNACK
WINE
BUTTE
MILK

!!
Cola
DONU
OREO

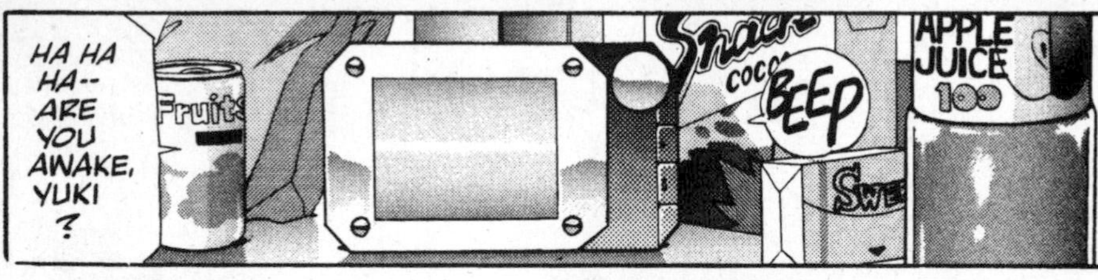
HA HA HA-- ARE YOU AWAKE, YUKI?
Fruits
COCO
BEEP
APPLE JUICE 100

KATSUMI...
Tee Hee
HA HA HA-- ARE YOU AWAKE, YUKI?
YOU WON'T GROW UP QUICKLY IF YOU DON'T EAT A LOT! ALSO, THE CHIEF GAVE YOU A WEEK OFF, SO TAKE IT EASY.
BUT I GUESS I REALLY SHOULDN'T EAT NOW.
RIGHT.
YOU WON'T GROW UP QUICKLY IF YOU DON'T EAT A LOT! ALSO,...

A WHOLE WEEK OFF!
WHAT'LL I DO?

HMMM...
!
THAT'S IT!

HEY! IF IT ISN'T YUKI!
WOW! IT'S BEEN SO LONG! WHAT'S HAPPENING?

UH... THE TRUTH IS, HIROKO, I'VE GOT THE WHOLE WEEK OFF.
AND I WAS THINKING, WHAT SHOULD I DO?
UH HUH. YOU PROBABLY SCREWED UP BIG TIME AT WORK, RIGHT?
WHAT?! NO WAY!
OKAY, OKAY-- SO WHAT KIND OF WORK ARE YOU DOING NOW, ANYWAY?

I MEAN, ANNAPPLE! ANNAPPLE JAPAN, GET IT? HA HA HA...
MY WORK? UM... I WORK AT AM...

I'M JUST WORKING AT THIS RUN-OF-THE-MILL SECURITIES FIRM.
YOU WORK AT THAT RISING CYBERNETIC HARDWARE COMPANY? WOW!

GOOD IDEA!
HEY, HIROKO, CAN I COME OVER?
HA HA-- IT'LL BE A LITTLE CLASS REUNION.
SURE! LET'S CALL DOUG AND ANNIE, TOO!

A REUNION, HUH...? FROM THAT PLACE...
SIGH
WELL, THEN-- WE'LL MEET IN FRONT OF MARUI DEPARTMENT STORE IN DISTRICT F-25 AT SEVEN.
OK!

KREAK
hff
OH, NO!
hff
I'M LATE! I'M LATE!
BEEP
BEEP
COME ON, LOCK!
AAAH!
WHAT TIME IS IT?
EEEK!
OH-MY-GAWD!

MARUI IN DISTRICT F-25! HURRY!
VROOM
I'M UNABLE TO GET ABOVE THE SPEED LIMIT. IS THAT ALL RIGHT?

I KNOW.
I JUST WANTED TO SAY IT.
YES, MISS.
PFSH
BUMP

VOOOM
HONK
HONK
ATARI

新発売
SSHHAA

MISS, I'M SORRY, BUT I THINK IT MIGHT BE BETTER IF YOU WALKED FROM HERE.
YEAH, I GUESS SO...
YUCK!
RAIN ON A DAY LIKE THIS. HOW DEPRESSING.
VMMM
SSHAAA
CHK
CHK
SPLUSH
SPLOOSH
Splash
AAH! FIFTEEN MINUTES LATE!
SSHAAA

SSHHAA
THEY'RE NOT HERE!
Hmpf!
VOOOM
HMM... IT'S JUST NOT LIKE HIROKO TO TAKE OFF JUST BECAUSE I'M LATE.

I WONDER IF SHE'S STILL AT HOME. BUT THE OTHERS HAVEN'T SHOWN UP YET, EITHER...
VUMM
SSHHAAA
I'D BETTER CHECK.
VMM
HELLO, THIS IS HIROKO SUZUKI. I'M NOT HOME RIGHT NOW, SO PLEASE LEAVE A VIDEO MESSAGE AT THE--
ABSENT

NOT HOME. DARN.
WHAT COULD'VE HAPPENED?
YUKI!
!

YOU'RE LATE! EVERYONE'S WAITING.
ANNIE!?

Z-Z-ZAP
IT'S BEEN...

SO...
LONG...

FWUMP

MY, MY... WHAT'S WRONG, YUKI ?
ANEMIA AGAIN?
EXCUSE ME. COULD SOMEONE PLEASE CALL ME A CAB?
SSHHAAA

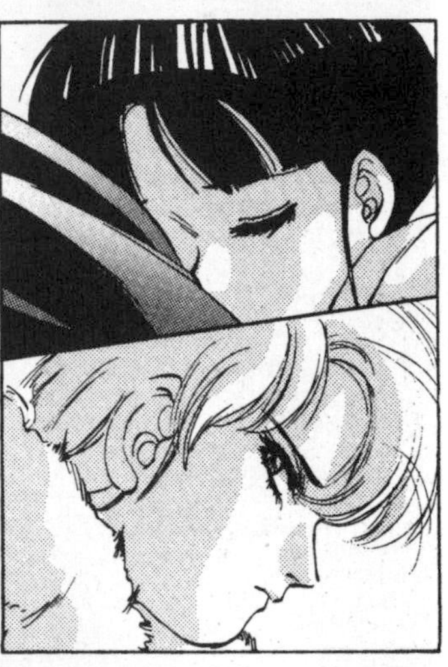

SSHHAAAA
VREE
VROOM

FALLING, FALLING...
INTO A DREAM, INTO THE NIGHT...
YUKI!
IN THE DARK, MY DREAM IS...
IN THE DARKNESS, MY LIFE IS...
--KI.
INTO A DREAM...
INTO THE NIGHT...
......
FALLING, FALLING.

Uhn...
YUKI! WAKE UP!

SO YOU'RE FINALLY WITH US AGAIN.
ANNIE !?

HIROKO ?
WHO... ?

PROFESSOR TAJIMA!?
IT'S BEEN A LONG WHILE, YUKI.

HEH... SLOW AS ALWAYS, HUH?
ZZ ZAP
THIS.
ANNIE?
WHERE AM I? DID... DID I PASS OUT AGAIN?

BUT... BUT, ANNIE...
WHY WOULD YOU DO SUCH A THING?
YOU STILL DON'T UNDERSTAND? THIS IS THE CLASS REUNION!
WE'LL DO IT JUST LIKE WE DID IN THE OLD DAYS, ONLY THIS TIME IT'S FOR ANNIE!
!?

YOU'RE GOING TO DIE, MISS LOSER.
FOR ME?

L-LIKE THE OLD DAYS... BUT THAT'S...
W-WAIT. ANNIE, WHERE ARE THE OTHERS? WHAT HAPPENED TO HIROKO AND DOUG?

FOR ME... TEE HEE...
THEY DIED!

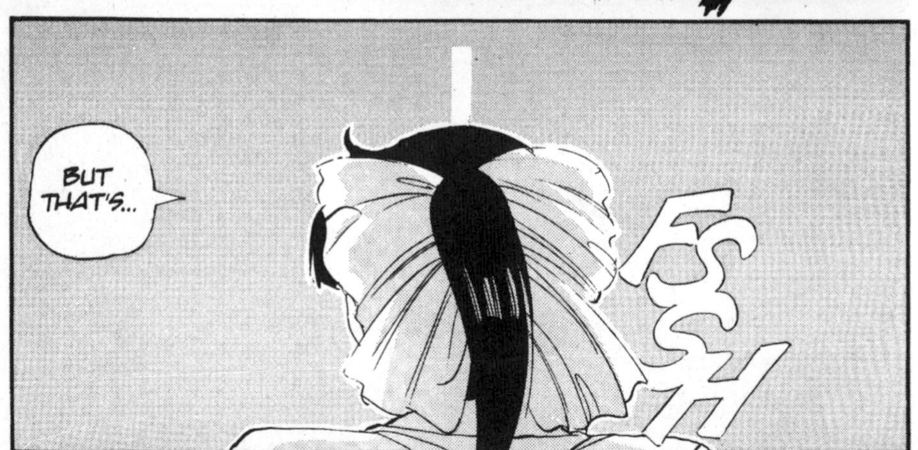
BUT THAT'S...
FSSH

AAH...
HIROKO, DOUG...
IT'S...
IT'S...
HORRIBLE...
HORRIBLE, ANNIE.
HORRIBLE...

WHAT A BORING WORLD IT IS...
...THESE DAYS.

AND THE ENTITIES ARE SO QUIET.
HAH! BUT WHEN THEY APPEAR, SHE DOESN'T KNOW WHAT TO DO WITH THEM!

WHO WOULDN'T KNOW WHAT TO DO?
HMPF! ARE YOU GOING TO MAKE ME SAY IT?

YES, YES--ENOUGH WITH THE COMEDY ROUTINE! TRY CLEANING UP THIS PLACE, WILL YOU?
COMEDY...
ROUTINE.

SIGH
I CLEAN AND CLEAN AND CLEAN, BUT YOU TURN AROUND AND MAKE A MESS AGAIN!

WHAT WAS THAT AGAIN!?
YOU GOT A PROBLEM!?

NOW I'M REALLY MAD!
WHAK
NO! AAH! STOP!
LET'S STRIP THE BIMBO! THAT'LL CURE HER ATTITUDE PROBLEM!
THUDD
WHAP
KEEP STILL!
.....

BONG
AH! STOP IT, PLEASE! WHAT ARE YOU DOING!
WUMP
NO!
SHADDAP!
KLONK
.....
WE'LL SEE YOU NEVER HOLD A BROOM AGAIN!
BEGONE, EVIL SPIRIT!
WHAK
WHO YOU CALLING AN EVIL SPIRIT!?

SHUT UP!!
KEEP IT QUIET!

OOPS! SORRY...
-Sigh-

WHAT'RE YOU DOING HERE, LEBIA?
WORK!
WORK!
THERE'S A LOT OF IT!
THUMP

AND YOUR TURN TO WORK IS COMING SOON!
SQUEEEK..
HO! WHAT KIND? WHAT KIND OF WORK?
WHEN IS IT? COME ON!

WILL YOU TWO SHUT UP!
CAN'T YOU SEE I'M BUSY!
Technics
SSSHHH

U... N...
YUKI... !

UH...
OH, NO! I CRIED MYSELF TO SLEEP...
KRIK
THIS IS NO TIME TO BE SLEEPING!

I'VE GOT TO FIND OUT WHAT'S GOING ON WITH ANNIE.

YUKI !
!

WHO'S THERE ?

......

STRANGE...
UMPF--
OF COURSE, IT WOULDN'T BE OPEN...

FSHH

IT... OPENED.
?

!!
THE DOOR TO YUKI'S ROOM HAS OPENED. BY ITSELF!
WHAT IS THIS?

PROFESSOR?
I DIDN'T DO ANYTHING!

IT COULDN'T BE... NOT HER!
NOT POWER LIKE THAT. THAT'S CRAZY!

HFF HFF... NO GOOD.
hff hff
IF I'D KNOWN THIS WOULD'VE HAPPENED... I'D HAVE EATEN.
hff
hff

YUKI...
hff
hff
hff
AGAIN !?

WHAT'S IN THAT ROOM ?
THERE AREN'T ANY OTHER DOORS.

!!!
OH MY GOD...

VVUMMMM
THIS IS...
UNBELIEVABLE!?

COULD THIS BE A GENE DRIVE SYSTEM... ?

THAT'S RIGHT, YUKI! BRINGS BACK OLD MEMORIES, DOESN'T IT? HEH HEH HEH
!
KLAK
SO THAT'S WHY THERE'S ONLY ONE DOOR.
VVVMMMMM
ANNIE!
ANNIE, YOU DIDN'T USE THIS TO...
BUT IT'S BECOME A LOT MORE COMPACT THAN IT USED TO BE...

HEE, HEE, HEE... HIROKO'S AND DOUG'S GENES HAVE ALREADY BEEN TRANSPLANTED INTO ME.
NOW IT'S YOUR TURN!
THAT'S HORRIBLE!
ANNIE, WHY? WHY'D YOU DO IT?!
HORRIBLE? DON'T MAKE ME LAUGH!
AREN'T WE THE PRODUCT OF SUCH PROGRAMS?
FLAP
SUCH "HORRIBLE" THINGS HAVE BEEN DONE TO US BEFORE, AND BY THE GOVERNMENT, NO LESS.

STOP! ANNIE!
YUKI! DON'T COVER YOUR EYES! DON'T COVER YOUR EARS! IT'S THE TRUTH!
WE WERE MADE TO BE ESPER WEAPONS!
NO, ANNIE... I'M NOT AN... ESPER WEAPON.
I'VE JUST GOT BETTER-THAN-AVERAGE INTUITION.
HA HA HA HA HA HA
YOU REALLY MAKE ME LAUGH! DON'T YOU SEE YOUR "INTUITION" IS THE RESULT OF OTHER PEOPLE'S GENES!

WHAP
AAH!

OUR NAMES AREN'T REAL!
STOP CALLING ME ANNIE!
A-ANNIE!
BACK IN THE OLD DAYS THOSE SCIENTISTS JUST MADE THEM UP AND GAVE THEM TO US!
STOP IT!
HA HA HA--
RIGHT, MISS B-007?

A LONG TIME AGO, BABIES WITH NO PARENTS WERE CHOSEN BY A COMPUTER AND PLACED IN THE ESPER PROJECT.
JUST... STOP IT... PLEASE!
AND WE WERE RAISED TO BE ESPER WEAPONS.
WE WERE GIVEN NUMBERS BASED ON OUR SECTIONS, AND EACH WAS IMPLANTED WITH GENES WITH DIFFERENT ABILITIES.

SO WHAT!? DOUG, HIROKO, AND I WERE LIVING HAPPILY... SO WHY? WHY?!
STOP, ANNIE!

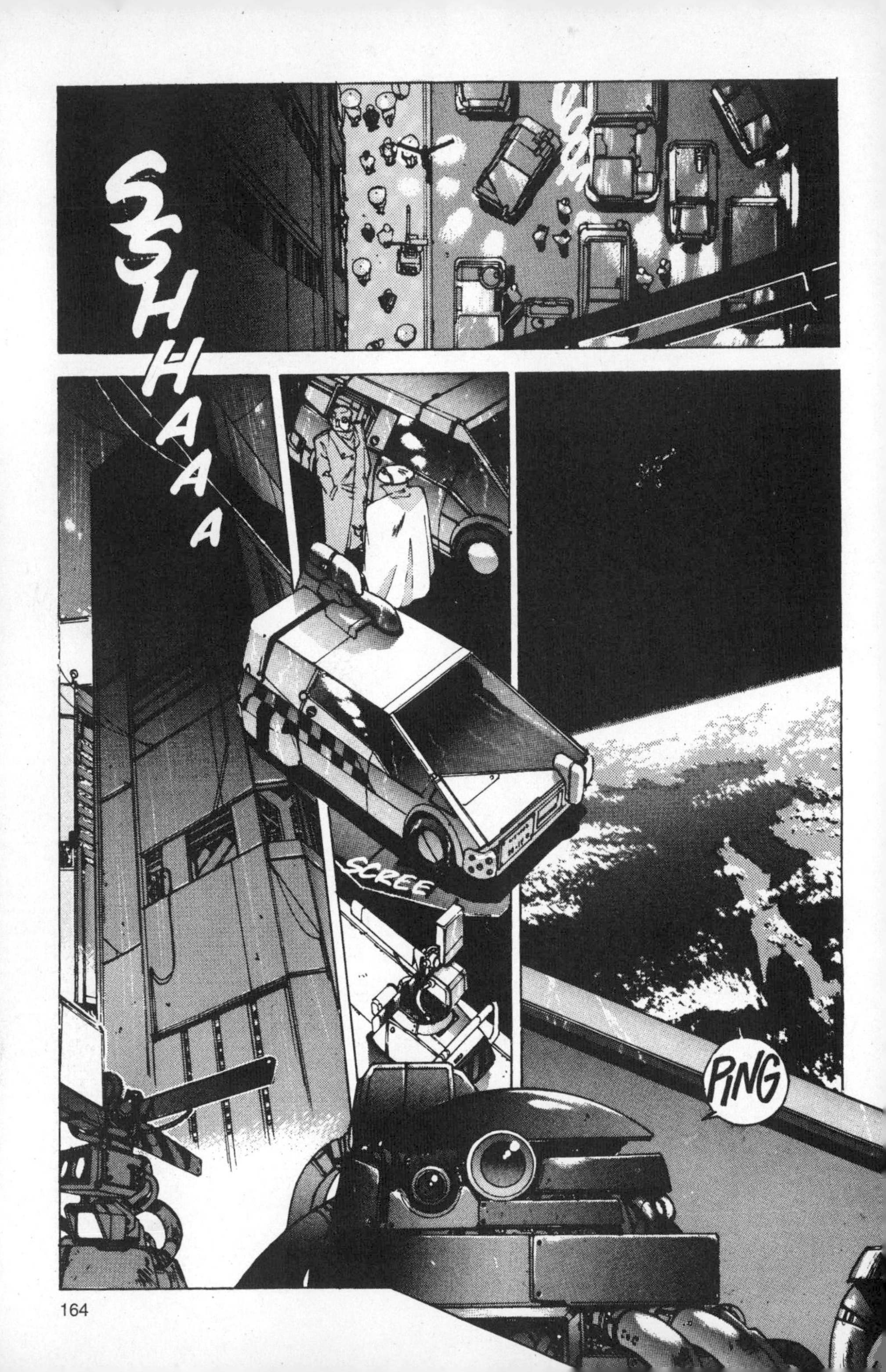
SSHHAAAA
SCREE
PING

HMMM
WHRR
DOOP
BEEP

HMMM... PROBABLY USING HER POWERS TO TAP INTO SOME COMPUTER NETWORK.
TAKA TAKA
BEEP
KATSUMI, WHAT'S LEBIA BEEN DOING ALL THIS TIME?

PFFT-- HOPELESS!.
WAAH HA HAHAHA!
MMM HMM. LEBIA WOULD STOP AT NOTHING, WOULDN'T SHE?
GETTING HER KICKS BY INPUTTING THE STOLEN DATA INTO HER OWN MACHINE, I'LL BET.

TIME FOR WORK, YOU TWO!
HA-- UH...

WHY ARE YOU INTERFERING WITH OUR LIVES?! WHY ARE YOU TRYING TO DESTROY THAT !?
ANNIE!?
YOUR LIVES? THEY'RE A SHAM!
AN ESPER WEAPON CAN NEVER LEAD A NORMAL LIFE!

AFTER ALL, WE'RE MUTANTS.

AAAH!
KDOOM

FSSSH
ANNIE! STOP IT!
SHOOM
BRRRRMM
THOOM
YIIII!

WHAT ARE YOU DOING, ANNIE?! STOP! YOU'LL DESTROY THE GENE DRIVE SYSTEM!

FUH
PROFESSOR... I'M GOING TO KILL THIS GIRL. SHE'S NO LONGER NEEDED, CORRECT?

...YEAH. I'LL PUT YOU AWAY, FOR GOOD!
.....
hff
hff
...UH...
ALL RIGHT.
...NOT AGAIN! WHO ARE YOU?!
YUKI
VRRRMBBL
FOOM
WHAT?
SHOOM

WHO IS IT?
ABSURD! THIS GIRL COULDN'T HAVE SUCH POWER...
IT COULDN'T BE!
BOOOSH
HIROKO. !?
WHUDD

IT WAS YOU WHO CALLED TO ME.
......
IT WAS YOU! WASN'T IT, HIROKO?
YUKI....

D-DAMN... SHE WAS SUPPOSED TO HAVE BEEN DEAD...
HMPF-- OH, WELL. MAKES NO DIFFERENCE NOW.
ANNIE!!!
TCH!
WHAT'S THE MATTER? DO YOU HATE ME? HA HA HA
!
FWAM

MISS B-007!
DIE BEFORE YOU EVEN HAVE TIME TO THINK ABOUT IT...

PING
KATHUDD
EEK
WAH!
AAAAH..

UH... AH...
NNGH!
KIDDY!
AH...
YUKI. IT'S A GOOD THING YOU WENT ON A DIET.
HOW DID YOU GET HERE?
DUEY. YOU DID A GREAT JOB TRACING HER. THANKS TO YOU, WE SAVED YUKI'S BUTT.
YES, MA'AM.

DUEY... ?
PARDON ME, MISS YUKI. I'VE BEEN TRACING YOUR MOVEMENTS FOR A WHILE.

WHY ?
WELL... YOU SEE...
WHO ARE THEY... ?
WHAT'S THEIR CONNECTION TO YUKI ?
NO MATTER. I'LL FINISH THEM OFF, TOO!
WE DISCOVERED THAT FOR THE LAST SEVERAL MONTHS, PEOPLE BELIEVED TO BE ESPER CHILDREN HAVE BEEN DISAPPEARING.
IT WOULDN'T BE... PROFESSOR TAJIMA...?
OF COURSE, THIS ISN'T THE JURISDICTION OF A.M.P. HOWEVER, TEN DAYS AGO, WE CONFIRMED THE IDENTITY OF THE GUILTY PARTY.
CD
DISCOUNT
VIDEO

BUT WE DID UNCOVER HIS CONNECTION TO YOU, MISS YUKI.
EVEN AFTER WE ACCESSED ALL COMMUNICATIONS NETWORKS!
THAT'S RIGHT. BUT WE DID NOT KNOW HIS LOCATION.
AND THAT'S WHY THE CHIEF GAVE ME A WHOLE WEEK OFF? WHY THAT'S...
SO THEN... WHAT? I WAS... BAIT?.
......
SSHHAA
YOU USED ME! DIDN'T YOU ?!
NO MATTER HOW OLD YOU GET, YOU STILL CAN'T DO ANYTHING BY YOURSELF. HEE HEE HEE
SO I'M NOTHING TO YOU, TO A.M.P.? I'M JUST A... A...
YUKI, TO THINK YOU WERE SAVED BY AN ACQUAINTANCE.
!

WHO THE HELL ARE YOU !?
SSHHAAAA
ANNIE...
FOR HER TO BE ABLE TO SAVE YOU FROM THAT FALL.
AND THAT POLICE UNIFORM... DOES THAT MEAN SHE'S NO ORDINARY PERSON?
FOOM
AND IF I'M NOT ?!
NOTHING AT ALL.
KZZZT
UH!
WHAMMM
THUDD
UNNGH!
WHAT THE HELL IS THIS ?!
HEH...

ANNIE...
WE'RE ALMOST THERE...
JUST A BIT MORE AND THE PROJECT WILL BE FINISHED.
AFTER TEN YEARS OF BEING STALLED, THE PERFECT ESPER WEAPON IS UPON US. FINALLY, OUR PROJECT WILL BE COMPLETED.
GOODBYE, YUKI, HIROKO, DOUG... YOU CHILDREN WHO PROVIDED ANNIE WITH YOUR GENES.
YOU WILL LIVE INSIDE ANNIE.
AS AN ESPER WEAPON!
YOU'VE GOT TO BE KIDDING! WHAT'RE YOU BABBLING ABOUT?

WHO !?
POLICE! YOU'RE OBVIOUSLY CRAZY, PROFESSOR TAJIMA. YOU'RE COMING WITH US.
FLIK
HEH HEH... CRAZY, YOU SAY?
ALL SCIENTISTS ARE CRAZY, YOU FOOL!
THAT'S HOW WE'RE ABLE TO THROW OURSELVES INTO OUR RESEARCH!
MY RESEARCH, AND ITS RESULTS, ARE THE PROOF OF MY EXISTENCE!
THAT DOESN'T MEAN IT'S ALL RIGHT TO MAKE VICTIMS OF YUKI AND THE OTHERS!
YOU'RE AN ACQUAINTANCE OF YUKI'S?

NOT AN ACQUAINTANCE! YUKI IS ONE OF US!
AND ONE OF MY MOST PRECIOUS FRIENDS!

YUKI? A COP?
IMPOSSIBLE...
PROFESSOR TAJIMA, YOUR PROJECT IS FINISHED. YOU'D BETTER GIVE UP, NOW!
INDEED, HEH HEH-- THAT MAY BE TRUE.
BUT THE PRODUCT OF MY RESEARCH IS ALREADY COMPLETE.
YOU MEAN ANNIE, OR WHATEVER HER NAME IS?

EXACTLY.
IN ANNIE, I SOUGHT THE ANSWER I NEEDED AS A SCIENTIST. AND ANNIE GAVE ME THAT.
WHAT?! AT THE EXPENSE OF YUKI AND THE OTHERS...?
CUT THE EGO CRAP!

AREN'T ALL HUMANS THAT WAY?
. . . . .
SHLEMP
I'VE MANAGED TO MAKE MY MARK ON HISTORY, SO I'M SATISFIED.
BEEP
IN THE FINAL ANALYSIS, WE ALWAYS PUT OURSELVES FIRST.
!!
W-WAIT!
HIROKO... DOUG... I'LL BE WITH YOU SOON.
GOODBYE, YUKI... ANNIE...
KADOOM
GAAH
PROFESSOR TAJIMA!!
!

DO YOU THINK DYING WILL SOLVE EVERYTHING... ?
.....

LET'S SING TOGETHER AGAIN. INSIDE A DREAM.
YUKI... ANNIE... HIROKO... DOUG

SSSHHH
DAMMIT! WHAT IS THIS?!
YOU BITCH!
SIT THERE AND WATCH YOUR ACQUAINTANCE DIE!
UNDERGROUND CABLES ARE PRETTY STRONG THESE DAYS, AREN'T THEY?

SHE'S NOT AN ACQUAINTANCE!
YUKI'S MY--
KIDDY!
YUKI-- !?

IT'S ALL RIGHT, KIDDY. YOU DON'T HAVE TO...
I'M JUST A BURDEN TO A.M.P. ANYWAY.
IDIOT! WHAT ARE YOU TALKING ABOUT !?

GO AHEAD... KILL ME, ANNIE. I'LL JOIN HIROKO AND DOUG, TOO.
EVEN IF I GO ON LIVING, THERE'S SO MUCH PAIN.
...THAT'S RIGHT.

YUKI!! CUT IT OUT! DON'T SAY THAT!

.....

KDOOM
WAAH!
EEE!
!!
AHH!
ZZZZZ
WHAT IS IT?!
HEE HEE HEE

ISN'T IT NICE? SO FLASHY!
ANNIE! STOP IT! THOSE ARE INNOCENT PEOPLE!

LOOK OUT!
SO WHAT? YOU THINK I CARE ABOUT THAT?
ANNIE!!
SSHHAAA
HEY! WHAT WAS THAT?!

THIS IS PATROL B-311
ZZZZ
EXPLOSION IN DISTRICT F-41 IN THE AREA OF 2-31-47. REPEAT
ANNIE...
SSHHAAAA
YUKI! YOUR GREATEST TRAGEDY IS THAT YOU DIDN'T HAVE A PREMONITION ABOUT TODAY, ISN'T IT?
TCH!
YUKI! RUN! IGNORE HER!
KRUNCH
AAAAH!
KIDDY!!!
WHAT-- ?!

YOU ONLY HAVE TO KILL ME, DON'T YOU? DON'T HARM ANYONE ELSE.
ANNIE! STOP IT! STOP IT! STOP IT!
GYAAH!
SHUT UP!
THWAK
AAH!

MY LITTLE SHOW HAS JUST BEGUN.
SS HHAAA
UHNN...
HEH HEH HEH... DON'T DIE YET, YUKI.

EVEN IF TOKYO'S NO GOOD, SOME OTHER CITY-STATE WILL ADOPT ME.
I'VE GOT TO DO IT WITH EVEN MORE FLASH AND GRANDEUR... HEE HEE

KZZT
NNGH!

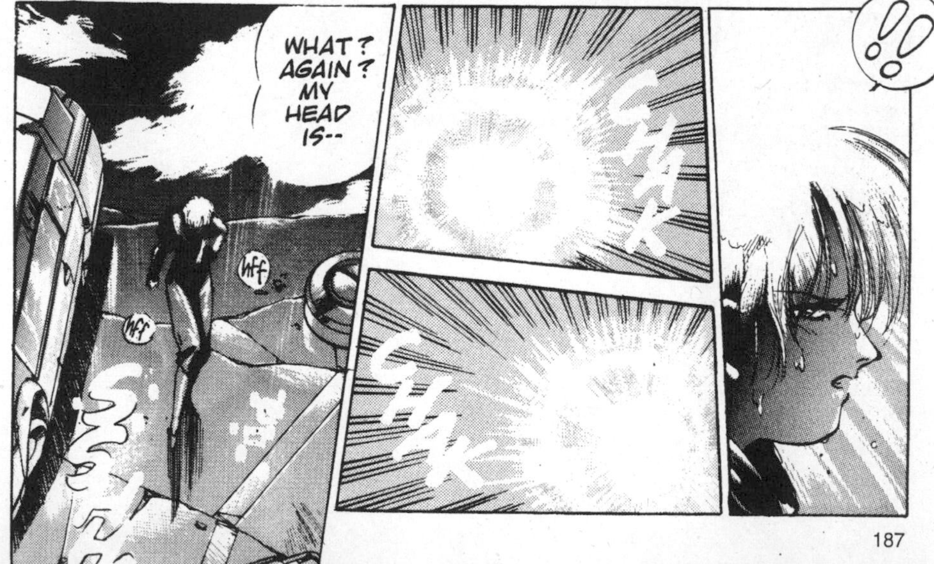
!!
CHAK
CHAK
WHAT? AGAIN? MY HEAD IS--
HFF
HFF

VOOM
VOOM

HMPF...
hff
hff
ESPER WEA-
PON ANNIE,
OR WHATEVER
YOUR NAME
IS!
GIVE
YOURSELF
UP QUIETLY!!
PROFESSOR
TAJIMA IS
DEAD!
VEEEE

PROFESSOR
TAJIMA?
HEH HEH
HEH--
SO WHAT?
TINK

KRUNCHH
EEAGH!

KADOOM

KADOOM
KADOOOM
!!
LOOK AWAY AND YOU'LL DIE!
!!
WHAT ?!
BRRUUMMM
HEE HEE HEE HEE
EEAAH!
WA!
hff
RETREAT !!
hff
HA HA HA HA!
RETREAT !
HELP !

!
ANNIE... PROFESSOR TAJIMA... HE'S... DEAD...
ANNIE...
hff
hff

EEAAAH!
WABOOM
KRAAKK
WHO CARES?! HIS ROLE IS FINISHED!
hff
hff
hff
I'M NOW A COMPLETE ESPER WEAPON!

GOODBYE, YUKI. HEH HEH HEH...
RRRMMBBB B
.....

WHAT?!
hff
hff
hff
THAT'S IMPOSS--

FALLING, FALLING
INTO A DREAM... INTO THE NIGHT...

GRR!
KOOOOM

VVVUUU
IN THE DARK, MY DREAM IS...
nff
nff
SHE'S PASSED OUT... BUT STILL STANDING!
WHAT'S--
IN THE DARKNESS, MY LIFE IS...
THAT SONG... STOP IT, YUKI!!

KDOOM
comics
FALLING, FALLING
DAMMIT! WHO!?
hff
hff
hff
WHO'S SHIELDING YUKI ?!
Guh-agh
INTO A DREAM...
SHUT UP !!
hff
Guh... ugngh...
HARULP
hff
I'LL BLOW YOUR HEAD OFF, BITCH!

STO-O-O-O-P!!
ANNIE!!

YUKI-I-I-I!!

KAZAAAT
GHAAH!

SO... THAT'S YUKI'S POWER...
THAT'S ABSURD! IT TURNED... RIGHT BACK ON ME!

YUKI... HA HA-- NOW I UNDERSTAND WHAT PRO-TECTED YOU ALL THIS... TIME...

IT WAS THE GENES OF HIROKO AND DOUG... INSIDE ME...

YUKI...
TWISTING MY... POWER...

ANNIE...
FWUMP
AS LONG AS I REMEMBER, YUKI... WAS ALWAYS... SO IMPORTANT... TO EVERYONE...
JUST BEING WITH YOU, YUKI...MADE EVERYONE FEEL...SO PEACEFUL...
MADE EVERYONE FEEL GENTLE AND KIND...
ANNIE, YOU SHOULDN'T TALK.
BECAUSE YOU SANG A SONG... WE ALL... USED TO SING TOGETHER.
THAT'S WHY EVERYONE... PROTECTED... YOU.
YUKI...
I'M SORRY... TO PUT YOU THROUGH THIS...
AS I REMEMBER THE OLD DAYS... YUKI.
I... CAN NOW JOIN THE OTHERS...
ANNIE!!

ANNIE, I'M THE ONE WHO SHOULD APOLOGIZE.

I LIED TO HIROKO AND DOUG, TOO.

IF I HAD ONLY TOLD THEM THE TRUTH THEN...

THAT I'M ACTUALLY A POLICE OFFICER...

THIS WOULDN'T HAVE HAPPENED.

AH...
LEBIA... KATSUMI... KIDDY... NAMI...

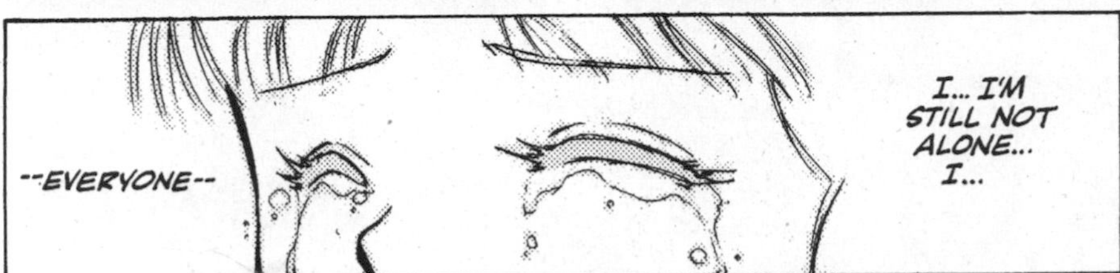
I... I'M STILL NOT ALONE... I...
--EVERYONE--

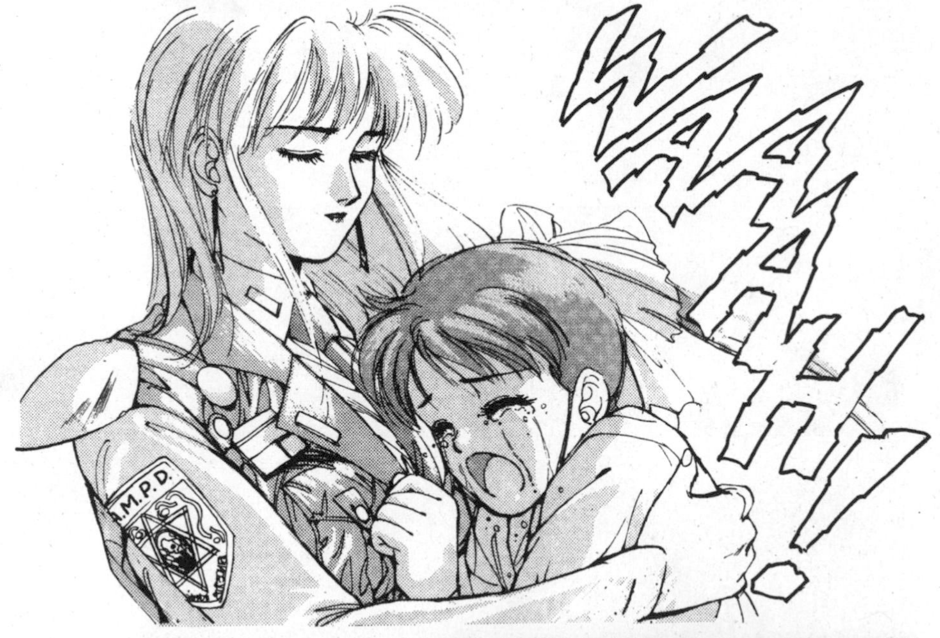
WAAAHH!

.....

YOU'VE GAINED EIGHT POUNDS ?
A DIE-E-E-ET ?
IT'S TRUE! WOW, KATSUMI-I-I !
PINCH
WELL, EVERYTHING JUST TASTES SO GOOD RECENTLY...
HUH
I THOUGHT I MIGHT TRY IT, TOO...

YUKI, WHY DON'T YOU TEACH THEM HOW TO DIET?
OUCH !
BONK
NAMI !
SURE...
HEE HEE

IF YOU LOOK TO YOUR LEFT YOU'LL UNDERSTAND.
I'M SORRY, MISS.
??
MY LEFT... ?

SPLASH
WHA--
!!

Ah!
WAIT A SECOND! WHAT THE HELL ARE YOU DOING?!
GOOD MORNING, LEBIA.

YAAAH!
-waah-
SEE... I TOLD YOU WE SHOULDN'T HAVE.
WHAT ARE WE DOING? ISN'T THAT OBVIOUS?
WHY?!
WH- WH--
BECAUSE IT'S SUMMER

WELL, YES... ACCORDING TO THE CALENDAR, IT'S SUMMER.
BUT DOES THAT MEAN YOU HAVE THE RIGHT TO COME INTO SOMEONE'S HOME UNINVITED, TURN UP THE HEAT, AND USE HER POOL?
POLICE
FOR CRYIN' OUT LOUD, HOW DID YOU GET IN?
WE ASKED DUEY TO GET YOUR "MONOLITH" TO OPEN THE DOOR FOR US.
DUEY?!
I'M SORRY, MA'AM.
POLICE
BESIDES, WHO ELSE HAS A POOL IN HER HOUSE?
KATSUMI, HOW MANY TIMES DO I HAVE TO TELL YOU?
HAVEN'T YOU LEARNED HIS NAME YET?
THAT'S LOUEY! LOUEY, OKAY?!
HE'S NOT A MONOLITH!

IF THAT'S NOT A MONOLITH, I DON'T KNOW WHAT IS.
AND THE SIZE AND COLOR...
YEAH, BUT JUDGING FROM THE SHAPE...
....
....
.....
I CREATED THREE ARTIFICIAL INTELLIGENCE DEVICES: HUEY, DUEY, AND FINALLY THIS HYPER-OPTIC TECHNOLOGY COMPUTER...
SPLISH
SPLOSH
SPLISH
UH...
NAMI, WHY DON'T YOU GET IN THE WATER ?
WELL, I... UM...
HEH, HEH...
...LOUEY. BUT NO ONE REMEMBERS HIS NAME.
THAP
YOU CAME TO SWIM, DIDN'T YOU ?
!!

SPLOOSH!!
gasp
haah
AH! COME TO THINK OF IT, NAMI...
SPLOOSH
I... CAN'T SWIM!
H-HELP!
THIS IS A GOOD OPPORTUNITY.
I'LL TEACH YOU HOW.
NOOOO!
SPLASH
kaff
kaff
DON'T CRY, NAMI. I'M SORRY...
I LOVE TAKING BATHS, BUT I CAN'T SWIM AT ALL!

LEBIA, WHY ARE YOU STANDING THERE WITH THAT DUMB LOOK ON YOUR FACE?
EH?
WELL, I WAS JUST THINKING IT MIGHT NOT BE SO BAD TO HAVE A DAY LIKE THIS...
keh--
ONCE IN A WHILE...
SPLOOSH

HUH ?!
WHAT THE HELL IS THIS?
WHAT'S WRONG, KATSUMI ?
TODAY'S PAYDAY, RIGHT? I JUST LOOKED AT MY ACCOUNT...
THERE'S A RECORD OF THE DEPOSIT...
BUT THREE MINUTES LATER, IT WAS WITHDRAWN !
WHAT !?

HMMM... IT'S THE SAME FOR EVERYONE.
THE MONEY WAS DEPOSITED AND, IMMEDIATELY AFTERWARD, WAS WITHDRAWN.
VVVMM

WHAT DOES THAT MEAN? IF IT DOESN'T COME BACK, WE DON'T GET PAID THIS MONTH?
CALM DOWN, KIDDY. ALL WE HAVE TO DO IS EXPLAIN WHAT HAPPENED AND WE'LL GET PAID AGAIN.
OH, I SEE.
DO YOU REALLY THINK THE CORPORATION MANAGING OUR POLICE FORCE IS THAT UNDERSTANDING?
THEY'RE MORE LIKELY TO SAY "YOU'VE ALREADY BEEN PAID."

WHAT?!
WELL, I MIGHT BE ABLE TO INFILTRATE THEIR COMPUTER SYSTEM AND REWRITE THE ACCOUNT.
AFTER ALL, MONEY THESE DAYS IS NOTHING BUT BITS OF DATA.

LOUEY, WHAT DO YOU THINK ?
PROCESSING--

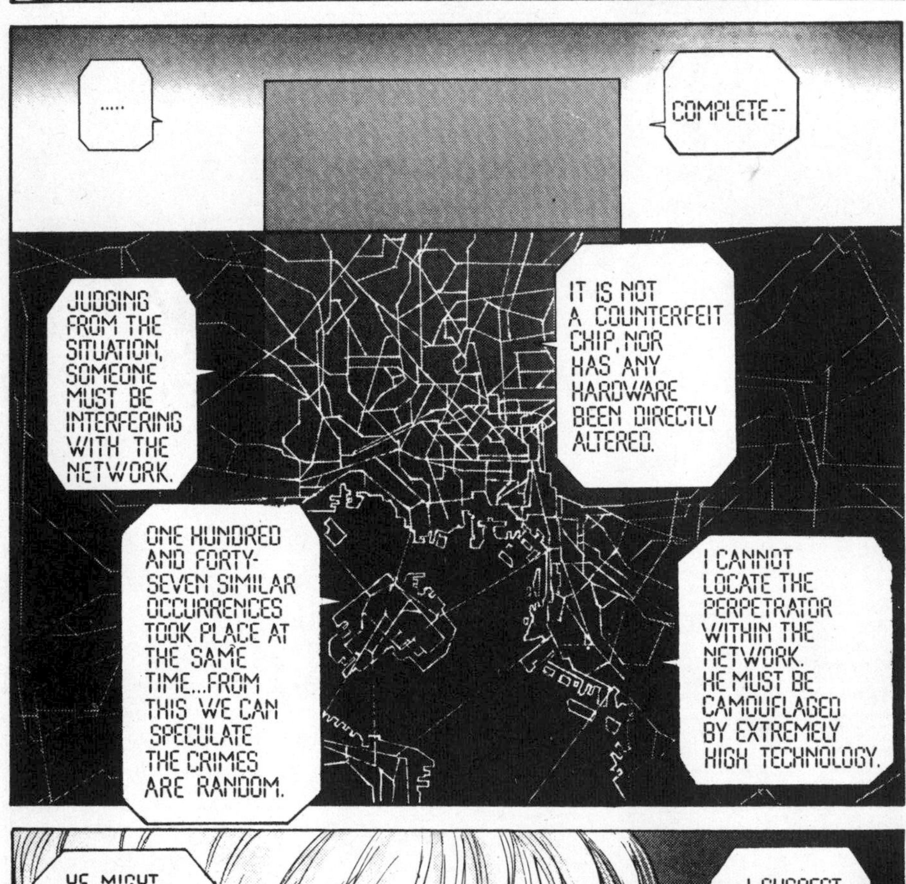
.....
COMPLETE--
JUDGING FROM THE SITUATION, SOMEONE MUST BE INTERFERING WITH THE NETWORK.
IT IS NOT A COUNTERFEIT CHIP, NOR HAS ANY HARDWARE BEEN DIRECTLY ALTERED.
ONE HUNDRED AND FORTY-SEVEN SIMILAR OCCURRENCES TOOK PLACE AT THE SAME TIME...FROM THIS WE CAN SPECULATE THE CRIMES ARE RANDOM.
I CANNOT LOCATE THE PERPETRATOR WITHIN THE NETWORK. HE MUST BE CAMOUFLAGED BY EXTREMELY HIGH TECHNOLOGY.

HE MIGHT EVENTUALLY TAMPER WITH THE ENTIRE CITY OF TOKYO.
I SUSPECT THAT IT COULD BE THAT LARGE A PROGRAM.

WELL, THEN...WHO HAS THE ABILITY TO DO SOMETHING LIKE THIS?
I DO NOT KNOW. NOT AT THIS POINT.
FORGET ABOUT THAT! WHAT ABOUT OUR PAY? HOW'RE WE SUPPOSED TO GET BY THIS MONTH?
Hee hee
THAT'S RIGHT, KATSUMI. AT THIS RATE YOU WON'T BE ABLE TO PAY ME BACK THAT MONEY YOU BORROWED LAST MONTH.
HUH? UM... WELL...
DUMMY. YOU'RE DIGGING YOUR OWN GRAVE.
ANYWAY, WE CAN'T JUST LEAVE THINGS LIKE THIS, CAN WE?
YUKI AND NAMI, YOU GO BACK TO HEADQUARTERS AND WAIT. KIDDY, YOU TELL CHIEF RALLY ABOUT THIS. KATSUMI, YOU'RE COMING WITH ME.
WHY ME?
THERE'S THE MATTER OF OUR PAY...
AND IF YOU CAN'T RETURN MY MONEY, I'LL HAVE YOU PAY WITH YOUR SERVICES. COME ON.

DOMINO'S PIZZA
21
WHISKY
LUCKY STRIKE
I.W.HARPER
RISA
Coke
BAR
KRMMBB
THIS IS JUNK CASTLE. THEY DEAL IN HARD DRUGS OVER HERE.
HEH HEH... THERE'S A SHOP HERE THAT BELONGS TO AN ACQUAINTANCE OF MINE.
!!
ACQUAINTANCE ?!
VRROOM
LEBIA, WHAT THE HELL... ?!

SSHHH

HERE IT IS.
CLUB
KIRIN
GIVE ME THAT
NEED MORE

YIKES!

THIS IS NO PLACE FOR THE LIKES OF YOU, WOMAN.

OR DID YOU COME HERE TO GET SLAMMED?

AND IF I DID?
!!

?
A... A...

LE--LEBIA MAVERICK...

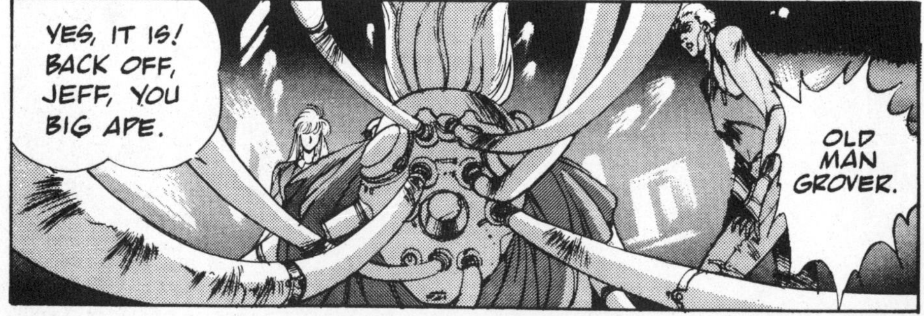
YES, IT IS! BACK OFF, JEFF, YOU BIG APE.
OLD MAN GROVER.

IT'S BEEN A LONG TIME, HASN'T IT LEBIA ?
HOW LONG HAS IT BEEN SINCE YOU STOPPED COMING AROUND HERE?

I GUESS ABOUT TWO YEARS, GROVER.
!?
I'VE COME TO ASK FOR YOUR HELP.

HA HA HA-- SOMEONE WITH YOUR TALENTS ASKING AN OLD MAN LIKE ME FOR HELP ?
IT'S NOT A LAUGHING MATTER, GROVER.
HMMM... COME WITH ME.
LET'S HEAR YOUR STORY, LEBIA.
SHUNT

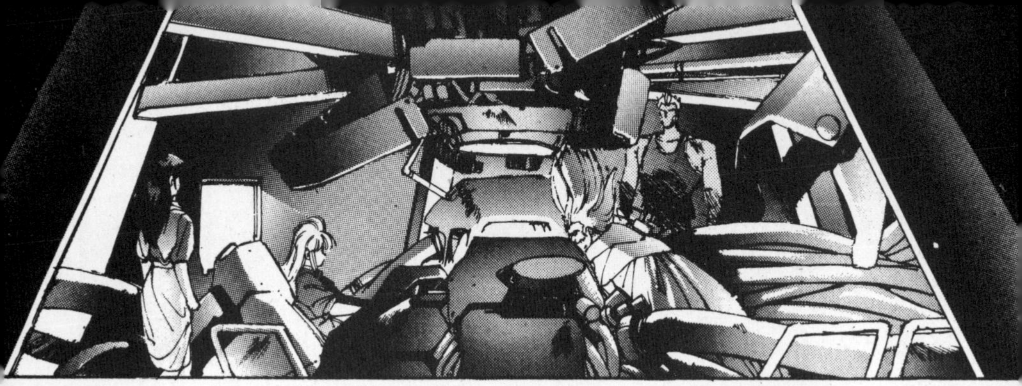

I SEE. YOU'LL NEED TO TAKE SOME OF THOSE.
THANKS, GROVER.

THAT'S LEBIA MAVERICK?
HEH HEH... YEP.
YOU'RE NOT EVEN IN THE SAME LEAGUE AS HER.
LEBIA...
.....

DRAGONFLIES: A VIRULENT COMPUTER VIRUS PROGRAM THAT REPRODUCES ITSELF QUICKLY.

ALL RIGHT! GO. DRAGON-FLIES!
VUN
KATSUMI, I CAN USE MAGIC, TOO. OF COURSE, I DO IT IN COMPUTER "LOGIC SPACE."
JUST AS YOU CHANT SPELLS WHEN YOU USE MAGIC, I USE EQUATIONS.
USING THEM, I CAN INVOKE MANY PROGRAMS.
THOSE PROGRAMS LET ME DO ANYTHING.
HEH HEH... INCLUDING ALCHEMY.

AND I CAN STEP RIGHT INTO THE WORLD OF LOGIC SPACE, ACTIVATING ALL FIVE SENSES THERE.
VARIOUS LINK SYSTEMS IMPLANTED IN MY BODY ALLOW ME TO DO WHAT NO NORMAL PERSON EVER COULD.
LEBIA...
FZZT

WHAT ?!
ZZZT
LOUEY!!
!!
ZZZT

I CLOSED ALL CIRCUITS 0.02 MILLISECONDS AFTER "IT" CAME IN.
Taka Taka
IT'S ALL RIGHT, MISS MAVERICK.
PING
HE SENT THE DRAGONFLIES RIGHT BACK AT ME.
HAH.
whew!
SSSSSS
BUT NOW I HAVE AN IDEA WHERE HE IS.
WHAT HAPPENED ?
EVEN SO, AT LEAST ONE PIECE OF HARDWARE'S SHOT.

UNFORTUNATELY, HE KNOWS WHERE WE ARE, TOO...
THAT CAN'T BE HELPED.
PING
LOUEY, START THE GUARDIAN PROGRAM.
FOR THE FIRST TIME IN A LONG TIME, I'M GOING TO THE OTHER WORLD, LOUEY.
YES, MISS. TAKE CARE.
VOOM
KATSUMI... DO YOU KNOW WHAT THEY CALL PEOPLE WHO DO THE THINGS I DO?
GOT ME.
VNN N
GROVER AND THE OTHERS ARE THE SAME BREED. WE ARE CALLED...
...VISIONAIRES.
I AM SPECIAL CLASS ALPHA VISIONAIRE LEBIA MAVERICK.

KRKK
KRRKKL
KRKKL
VOOOM
KDOOM
KBOOM
KRAKK

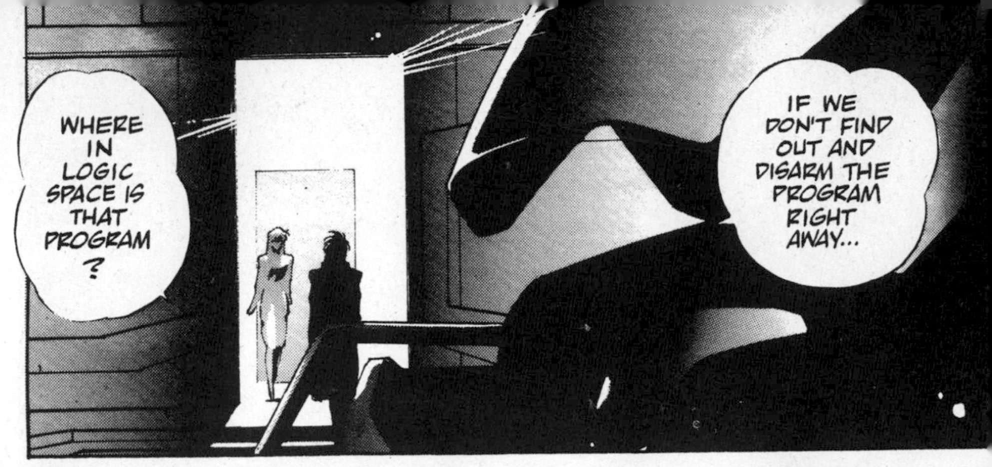
WHERE IN LOGIC SPACE IS THAT PROGRAM ?
IF WE DON'T FIND OUT AND DISARM THE PROGRAM RIGHT AWAY...

...THERE'S NO TELLING WHAT MIGHT HAPPEN.
PING
NOW, THEN...

Joyous journey, engine on fire.
Ready to go! It'll be all right.
Calling Crystal Girl.

LEBIA! IS THIS ANYTIME TO BE SINGING ?
We'll all tune up!
KACHIKK
HA HA-- KATSUMI, WHEN I FIND THE PROGRAM IN LOGIC SPACE...

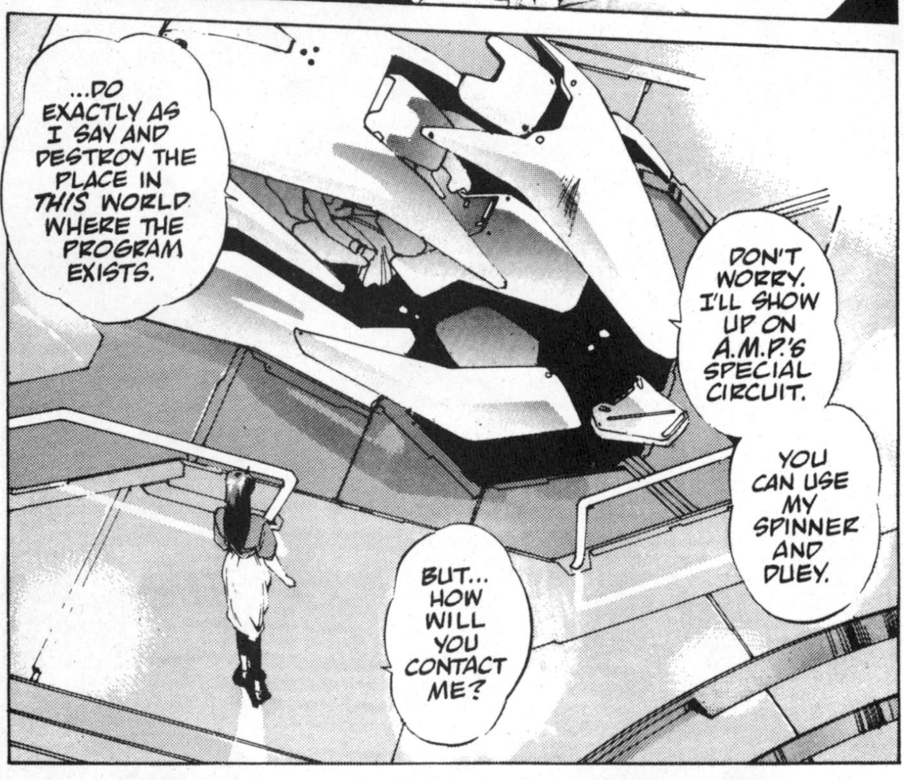
...DO EXACTLY AS I SAY AND DESTROY THE PLACE IN THIS WORLD WHERE THE PROGRAM EXISTS.
DON'T WORRY. I'LL SHOW UP ON A.M.P.'S SPECIAL CIRCUIT.
YOU CAN USE MY SPINNER AND DUEY.
BUT... HOW WILL YOU CONTACT ME?

RIGHT. IT'S ABOUT TIME TO GO.
LOUEY, BEGIN ELECTRONIC CONVERSION.
YES, MISS.

SIGHT CONVERSION
PROCESSING
FSSHU
CLEAR

FSSHU
HEARING CONVERSION

CLEAR
SMELL CONVERSION
FSSHU
SHUNT
CLEAR

FOOM!!
LOUEY! STOP CONVERSION! CLOSE SYSTEM!
SHOOM
YES, MA'AM
hff!
hff!
hff!
hff!
WHAT HAPPENED, LEBIA?
LOUEY! WHAT HAPPENED WITH THE GUARDIAN SOFTWARE? I WAS BEING INTERCEPTED BY ANOTHER PROGRAM!
THE GUARDIAN SOFTWARE IS IN OPERATION. THAT PROGRAM MAY HAVE BROKEN THROUGH THE GUARDIAN...

IT LOOKS LIKE MY OPPONENT HAS A LOT MORE POWER THAN I IMAGINED.
SHUN
OH, BOY...
LEBIA... ?
HEH HEH...
LET'S DO IT ONE MORE TIME, LOUEY!
YES, MA'AM.

SWITCH OFF ALL CIRCUITS IN THIS ROOM FROM THE OUTSIDE NETWORK.
UNDERSTOOD, MISS LEBIA.
RECONNECT THE CIRCUITS WHEN THE ELECTRONIC CONVERSION IS COMPLETE.

LEBIA, YOU ACTUALLY LOOK EXCITED.
I'M COUNTING ON YOU, KATSUMI.

YEAH!

PIONEER
SUNTRY BRANDY V.S.O.P.
POLICE 66
WEEOOOO
HMMM...
YOU'RE SURE THAT'S WHAT LEBIA SAID?
VOOM
YES, CHIEF RALLY.
AND YUKI, YOU TRY TO MONITOR ANYTHING THAT GOES ON IN THE NETWORK.
OKAY, KIDDY. I'LL TRY AND VERIFY THAT FROM HERE.

A MESSAGE MIGHT COME IN FROM KATSUMI OR LEBIA, SO WAIT FOR IT.
KIDDY AND NAMI, STAND BY FOR ORDERS.
YES, MA'AM!
BEEP

IT WOULD EVEN SEEM CUTE IF ALL THE PROGRAM DID WAS INTERFERE WITH BANK ACCOUNTS.
BUT I DON'T THINK THAT'LL BE THE CASE.

BUT WHO WOULD CREATE SUCH A PROGRAM... AND WHY?
ONE FALSE MOVE, AND THE ENTIRE TOKYO SYSTEM COULD BE LOST.

IS THIS ANOTHER CITY-STATE'S WEAPON?
WHAT IS IT...?
VURRR

TOUCH CONVERSION
LATER, KATSUMI.
SHOOM
CLEAR
OPEN SYSTEM
LEBIA...

NARUSE HEAVY INDUSTRIES

!

THE DATA'S UP AND DISAPPEARED AND I CAN'T RETRIEVE IT NO MATTER HOW MANY TIMES I TRY!
WELL... UH...
WHAT'S WRONG?
I'M SERIOUS!
THERE YOU GO AGAIN.

UHN!

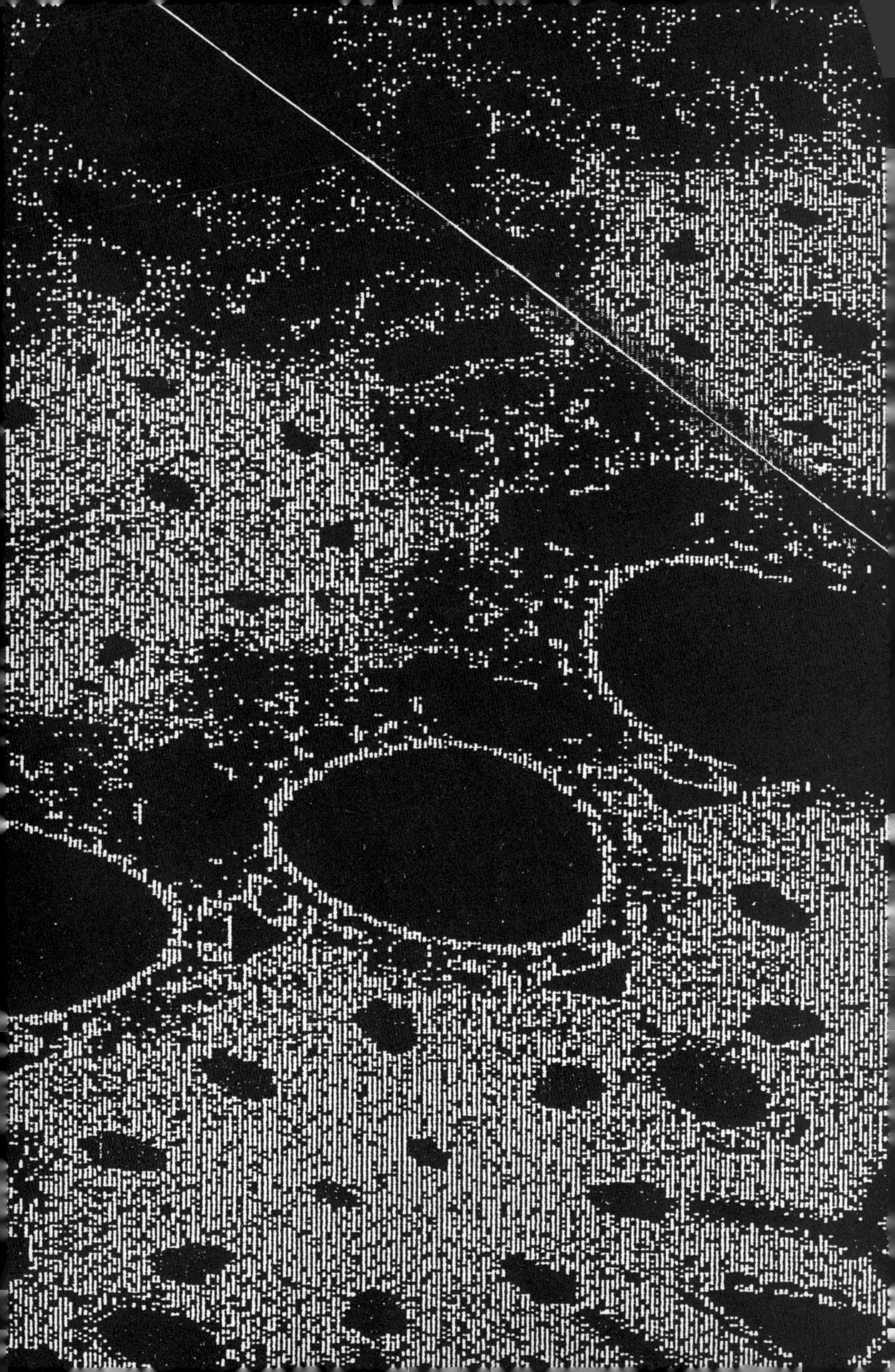

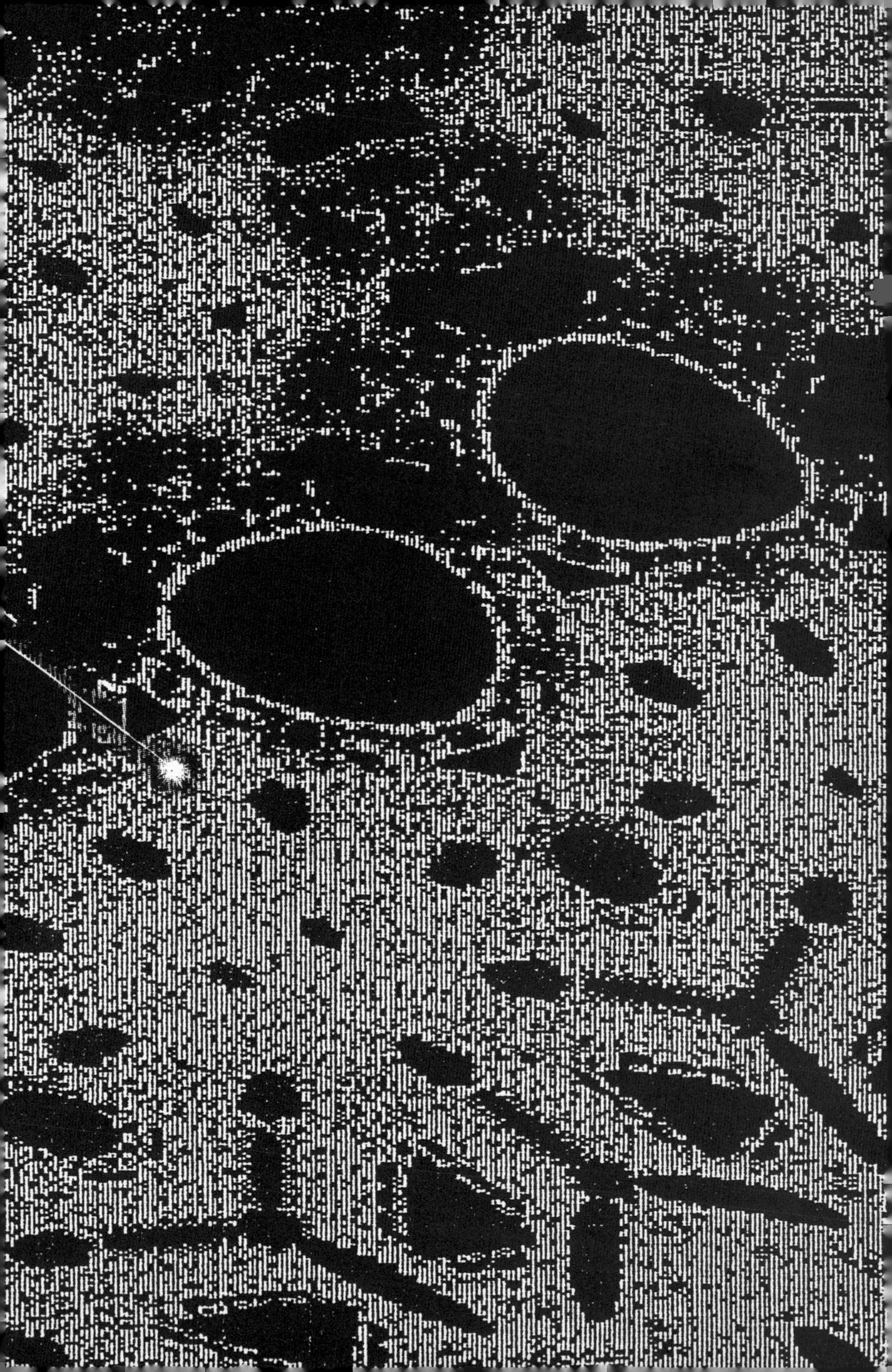

SHUM

SO FAR SO GOOD.
FSSHHH
WHEW!

BUT I CAN'T GET COM-FORTABLE LOOKING LIKE THIS.
NOT BAD, LOUEY.
HOW IS IT, MISS LEBIA?
WHOOSH
MUCH BETTER.

RRMMBB
!?
RRRMMMMBBB
!! WHAT--?! THE DATA COLONIES ARE DISAPPEARING... NO, THEY'RE BEING ABSORBED!
IT'S NOT JUST BITS AND PIECES OF DATA, IT'S EATING THE WHOLE NETWORK!

RRMMMBB

THAT'S THE MESSAGE FROM KATSUMI, CHIEF.
TELL KATSUMI TO RETURN TO HEADQUARTERS. KIDDY, YOU TRACE LEBIA.
CHIEF, WH-WHAT ABOUT ME...?
NAMI, WE CAN'T GET CAUGHT UP IN THIS.
THERE'S STILL SOME ENTITY SURVEIL-LANCE TO GET DONE.
YES, MA'AM.
CHIEF! A REPORT'S JUST COME IN THAT SOME CONGLOMERATES HAVE LOST THEIR ENTIRE DATABANKS!
WHAT!?
WHICH COMPANIES?
AT THIS POINT, FOUR. LIQUID ENTERPRISES, NARUSE HEAVY INDUSTRIES, AKITAKA MOBILECRAFT, AND SUMI PHARMACEUTICALS!
YUKI, PUT THE MAP ON THE MONITOR.
YES, MA'AM.

HMMM...THERE DOESN'T SEEM TO BE ANY CONNECTION BETWEEN THE COMPANIES THEMSELVES...

IT'S THAT PROGRAM.
YUKI, IF IT WERE TO WIPE OUT THE DATA OF ALL THE OTHER COMPANIES IN TOKYO, HOW LONG WOULD IT TAKE?

AT THIS RATE, EVERYTHING WOULD BE GONE IN 23 HOURS, 17 MINUTES, AND 41 SECONDS.
TWENTY-THREE HOURS...
...UNTIL TOKYO DIES.

To be continued....